ESSENTIAL
SCULLING

ESSENTIAL SCULLING

DANIEL J. BOYNE

GUILFORD, CONNECTICUT
AN IMPRINT OF THE GLOBE PEQUOT PRESS

Published by The Globe Pequot Press
Previously published by The Lyons Press

The Lyons Press is an imprint of The Globe Pequot Press.

Designed by Compset, Inc.

Illustrations © Ellen Kennelly

Photo credits:
pg. viii and pg. 24 © by Mary Lee
pg. xiv © by M.L. Thomas
pg. 8 and pg. 110 © by Joe Wrinn
pg. 44 and pg. 126 © by Jon Chase
pg. 60 © by David Foster
pg. 74 © by Leslie Stout
pg. 90 © by Joel W. Rogers

Library of Congress Cataloging-in-Publication Data

Boyne, Daniel J.
    Essential sculling / Daniel J. Boyne.
        p.   cm.
    Includes index.
    ISBN 1-55821-709-6
    1. Rowing. I. Title.
GV791.B69 2000
797.1'23—dc21   00-027370

Manufactured in Canada
First edition/Third printing

*To all my students, who have
provided the pages of this book
and many good memories.*

CONTENTS

The author teaching with his daughter in tow.

PREFACE

In the summer of 1978, my sports-minded sister got me into something new. She'd just returned from her first year at Mount Holyoke College with a mouthful of strange "crew" jargon. The new rage on campus was rowing, and she was completely taken with it. In fact, she planned to row straight through the summer by joining a local club. Naturally, she would need a training partner.

I had nothing better to do, having just suffered through a rather anticlimactic high school graduation. Besides, I knew I had little choice. The same recruiting drive had happened once before, when Shawn had gotten involved with cross-country running. As her younger brother, I knew there was no escape. I'd become a runner; now I was to row.

More so than most activities that I got myself into, my sister's choices were always a bit spartan. The rowing business proved to be no exception. In fact, with its many ascetic demands, it appeared to be a perfect form of ritualized self-punishment. The first requirement was to wake up at 5:00 A.M., so we could drive out to the boathouse and be under way by sunrise. The lake was generally calmer then, devoid of powerboats and other wake-producing nuisances.

Sleepy-eyed, I began my sculling lessons. Single sculls were one-person boats, as opposed to the eight- or four-person sweeps that my sister had rowed at Mount Holyoke. In those boats, each rower held a single, twelve-and-a-half-foot oar. The oars in sculling boats were still fairly long, but short and tapered enough to allow for control in each hand. Still, the overall body motion was similar, and Shawn easily made the transition from sweep rowing to sculling.

She was put in a sleek, ten-inch-wide shell, which seemed to skim over the water like a flying carpet. I was put into a wherry, a shorter, stouter craft, which in comparison looked and behaved more like a camel. I was shown how to get in and out of the boat, told to use my legs when rowing and to keep my left hand slightly higher than my right. How absurd, I thought to myself, that one's hands had to overlap in the first place. And what was this silly business with a sliding seat?

Somehow, I overcame my initial suspicions with these odd encumbrances and ventured out onto the still lake. Like most brothers, I assumed that if my sister could do something, it would certainly be a cinch. This was the first of many wrong assumptions. Shoved out onto the water like a child forced to swim, I took my first tentative strokes, first just using my arms and back to get used to the strange crossover and feathering motion my hands had to make. The boat putted along, and all seemed well enough.

Then I tried to make sense of the sliding seat, which extended the length of the stroke and theoretically allowed one's legs to be employed. The wherry protested at this effort. One of my oars dug deep and the boat quickly pitched to that side, nearly dumping me into the lake. I stopped, a little shaken, and tried to begin again. The next attempt was better for a while, but then I started paying too much attention to my oar blades and my hands began to knock against each other. Toward the end of the outing I had bloody knuckles, and to top off the morning, my seat came off the runners just as I was trying to pull into the dock. I rammed the little makeshift pier head-on, feeling not unlike the hapless Mr. Toad in *The Wind in the Willows*.

The boat was simply not behaving. Instead of carrying me like a good beast of burden, it bucked and tried to throw me off balance. During my next few outings, I gripped the oars more firmly, stiffened my resolve, and decided to apply a little more brute force. This decision proved to be foolish, however, for the more rigidly I tried to bend the boat to my will, the more it rebelled. It was not the boat that needed breaking in, it was me.

The coach, an elderly British man of some repute in rowing circles, didn't seem to take much note of my antics. I'd spot him across the lake occasionally, trailing a group of experienced scullers. Because of his bushy white mustache and his big barrel chest I secretly nicknamed him "The General." His philosophy, I came to find, was that the basics of sculling were best learned through a process of self-discovery (i.e., trial and error). Once in a while he would motor by me, shouting something incomprehensible like, "Don't shoot your tail!" Later, after another more or less frustrating morning, my sister would translate these remarks for me.

"Don't worry," she assured me. Soon, when I graduated into a real single, all of my problems would disappear. The wherries were just junky practice boats, and everyone did poorly in them. Hearing this, my pride was temporarily restored, and I struggled my way through the wherry initiation period. By the end of two weeks, I was still having some problems with balance and steering, but I'd managed to keep dry, and luckily no one had seen me run aground on the little island in the middle of the lake.

Encouraged by my sister, I asked The General if I could move into a "real" single. "Do you think you're ready?" he asked me. I saw him glance down at the bloody scrape on my right hand, and I made no effort to hide it. Perhaps it would impress him, I thought, my little red badge of courage.

"Sure," I replied. "I think I'm ready." He nodded slowly. "As you like," he said rather too casually, as if it were no big deal. But I knew better, of course, having been filled in by my sister. Soon I'd be flying along with ease, finally rid of my ornery camel boat. Doing well was all a matter of getting good equipment and moving into the coach's inner circle. Now that I'd persuaded him to give me a chance, it was up to me to make a good impression.

So began my first trip in a real single. I paddled away from the dock, arms only, just as I had my first time in the wherry. The boat indeed felt much more responsive, some ways for better, some ways for worse. It certainly went much faster, without as much effort on my part, but it was also a lot less forgiving. I reached this conclusion just a stone's throw from the dock when I took a deep stroke with my starboard oar and got pitched neatly into the lake.

I surfaced, unscathed, but a little disoriented. It all happened so fast that my mind felt a step behind my body. My boat was still floating upright, as if nothing had happened, but I was somehow no longer in it. Naturally, my first instinct was to get back in, but I soon found that this wasn't so easily done without the use of a dock. I looked around me but not a soul was to be seen, so I floated hopelessly beside the shell and started to go over my options. I had just decided to try to swim ashore when The General suddenly appeared in his ridiculous little launch.

"Caught a crab, did you?" he said dryly. I was silent, wondering whether he had come over to offer assistance or to upbraid me with some weird British wit. As we motored back to the dock, with the single in tow, I desperately tried to figure out what had happened, and what it meant to "catch a crab." Later that morning, my sister explained it to me, and I held less of a grudge against The General. Instead I began to reassess my own approach to the sport, my overambitious expectations. I decided to go back to the wherry for a while, and return to the real single when I was ready to handle it well.

In the years that followed, I eventually figured out how to scull more and more proficiently under the erratic tutelage of various coaches and veteran scullers. While I never intended to become a sculling instructor, this circuitous, hard-won route to learning the sport inadvertently prepared me for just that job. In short, I knew all the mistakes to be made, because I had made most of them my-self. When I was asked to serve as the director of the recreational sculling program at Harvard University, I confessed to Harvard Crew Coach Harry Parker that I really wasn't an expert on sculling. "Don't worry," he said. "No one is." The final irony came shortly thereafter, when I learned that my post at Weld Boathouse had once been held by none other than The General himself, a man named Ernest Arlett.

Nearly a hundred years old, Weld Boathouse has been, and continues to be, a mecca for American scullers testing their wings. In the summer alone, nearly a hundred scullers pass through its doors daily, all needing different levels of attention and advice. Although I had gained an intuitive sense of sculling prior to entering Weld, it was only when I had to articulate and format this information to such a volume of students that my real knowledge of the sport began. With so many students, I also began to appreciate why The General had become so sparse with his comments.

This book has grown out of over a decade of teaching thousands of different scullers with diverse backgrounds and goals, and another decade before that learning the art of sculling on my own. Unwittingly or not, my students have also been my teachers, and they are embedded in the pages of this book. I have also been fortunate to work on the Charles River, alongside of some of the most knowledgeable coaches and rowers in the country.

I wrote this book largely in response to the demands of my students, who frequently complain that too little is written about the sport of sculling. "Don't read," I sometimes tease them, "just do." Over the years, however, I had actually thought about writing such a how-to book, but had always hesitated for a few reasons. One is the above-mentioned belief that you can't learn a physical activity from a book, no matter how many nice words or pictures it contains. The second was that I felt like I was still learning more about the sport year after year, row after row, student after student. The last hesitation was that sculling is one of those sports in which the more specific you get about methodology, the more you open yourself up to debate.

Within the word *essential* lies the word *essence*. In the writing of this book, I wanted to provide not only the specific information you need to know to become a better sculler but something a little more. In a way, my writing process became a little like the process of learning to scull—first getting caught up in all the various details related to equipment, technique, physiology, and the like. As time went by, these became somewhat secondary to the goal of trying to express the true essence of the sport, the pure joy of moving over water feeling unencumbered by superficial concerns.

Throughout the book, I make an effort to sketch out the personality of the sculler, one who does not mind being alone on the river, or for that matter in their other pursuits. *Self-motivated* is the word that most often comes to mind. Still, even if scullers share certain traits, they often have different ways of learning and diverse goals. While it is difficult not to express some specific thoughts on proper technique, I tried to steer away from absolute truths, which would deprive the reader from developing their own sense of style. In terms of goals, many books on rowing or other sports assume either a purely competitive or a purely recreational focus, and construct an artificial divide between the two groups. The beauty of rowing is that such a line is self-imposed; competitiveness depends largely on how much time and effort you want to put in.

Sculling is learned in seasons, as the saying goes. And while a book has its own limitations as a teaching tool, I still believe that reading is one of the most effective ways to understand sophisticated concepts. Reading allows you to progress at your own rate, to turn down the page when you've had enough. In this way, sculling and reading are similar in that they are contemplative acts. It is no great surprise, then, that many of the best scullers I know are chronic thinkers, always analyzing and debating ideas about technique, rigging, and physiology in order to reinterpret old knowledge and apply it freshly to their own efforts.

Daniel J. Boyne
Weld Boathouse

The boathouse in winter. A time for reflection.

CHAPTER 1

PREWATER CONSIDERATIONS

To the outsider, sculling is an act of mysterious beauty. The graceful, rhythmic motion of the oars through the water, the silent, smooth glide of the narrow shell. Many people who don't row often falsely perceive it as an esoteric, elitist activity, a form of water ballet that requires years of hard training, private lessons, and unique physical gifts. Conversely, some assume that sculling is no more difficult than rowing a dingy. Most of these misconceptions stem from the fact that until recently, the practice of sculling has occurred largely out of the public eye, overshadowed by more popular sports and restricted to private institutions.

Who is the sculler? What sort of person takes to this odd sport where one sits backward and repeats the exact same motion, again and again? Indeed, the repetitive movements and backward-facing stance of the sculler suggest one or two things about the general character of the sculler and the paradoxical nature of the sport. Blindly determined, independent, completely obsessed? Yes, yes, maybe. But about what? Health and heart-rate measurements? Olympic victory? Just being on the water and not flipping? Whatever the goal, perhaps the most powerful suggestion inherent in the sculling motion is that what lies ahead is less important than the motion itself, of keeping focused on the immediacy of the moment. The goal is ahead, known, but not seen. Out of necessity, it is inwardly perceived.

I often tell beginning students about my own ungainly entry into the sport, both to put them at ease and to reaffirm that learning how to scull can indeed be more a trial of one's patience and inner resolve than a test of one's physical ability. I also tell my story to illustrate several common preconceptions that novices often bring with them when they show up for their first row. Some of these have to do with the physical aspects of the sport, like fitness, equipment, and technique. Others have to do with things like attitude and coaching style. Before you learn anything about sculling, you should leave as many of these preconceptions as possible on dry land, so they won't impede your progress on the water.

Although I'll cover some of these areas in greater detail in later chapters, here are some of the initial misconceptions that the newcomer to sculling must often first address.

HEALTH AND FITNESS

Many books and articles present rowing as the ultimate form of exercise. Numerous studies over the years have tried to assess the beneficial effects of rowing in areas ranging from cardiovascular fitness and cholesterol levels to longevity and quality of life. The most amusing one I've ever heard of was a 1904 study of former Harvard crew members which asserted that they were more likely than other athletes to get married and have children.

Row if you like to row, and let the rest take care of itself. Yes, rowing clearly offers some wonderful physical and mental benefits, but there are also some limitations to realize beforehand. First, while you don't need to possess the fitness level of an Olympic athlete to row, you do need to be in reasonably good shape. Aerobically, rowing is one of the most demanding exercises around, rivaled only by cross-country skiing in terms of the cardiovascular effort it requires. If you don't already exercise on a regular basis, take it easy with your rowing until your body gets used to the new demands. Naturally, if you have any concerns about your health, get a preliminary checkup with your doctor.

Another popular claim is that sculling is a low-impact sport, providing a gentle means of exercise that doesn't aggravate the joints. It is sometimes compared to swimming, because both activities work with water. To ex-runners, who have pounded their knees too long on the pavement, rowing looks appealing as a viable replacement. But water can be hard too, depending on how hard you work against it. Rowers have their own set of injuries. Find an ex-Olympian or national team rower without a back problem and you have found a lucky one. The other common overuse injury is to the intercostal muscles around the rib cage.

If you have a back problem, take it easy and see how the rowing motion affects your body. Done in moderation, sculling may help strengthen your back; done poorly or excessively, it may aggravate it. If you have no physical ailments, at least be aware of the added strain on the torso area and, as you progress in the sport, develop a strengthening plan, which will serve as a preventative against such injuries.

Lastly, try not to pin all your hopes and dreams on rowing as the single ingredient for a good life. It is a wonderful sport, to be sure, but it doesn't need to become the whole focus of your existence. I mention this because many novices, especially those who are younger, can begin to develop an almost addictive behavior toward competitive rowing that isn't healthy either mentally or physically. Again, moderation is the key.

AGE

Ever wonder why your fifteen-year-old son or daughter seems to be learning a lot faster than you, or why that old guy in the next boat over, the one pushing eighty, leaves you in his wake? Sculling honors both youth and experience. The paradox of the sport is that it can be learned and enjoyed in an hour or less, yet its subtleties require several seasons, if not years, to master.

Many young people have the ability to watch and imitate the sculling motion, without feeling self-conscious or thinking too hard about it. An adult learner says, "Wait a minute, I've got to think about this first," while a younger person, particularly one with less caution or inhibition, dives right in. It's the same with many physical activities: kids sometimes get off to a definite advantage because of their spontaneity, fearlessness, and lack of concern about being able to analyze things as they do them.

The difference with sculling, I've found, is that (inevitably) adults eventually advance further by putting their analytical skills and mental discipline to work. This is how veteran scullers become so efficient. Most have developed their skills through the twin virtues of cunning and patience. So relax. Depending on your fitness level, intelligence, and patience, you will eventually catch up to your kids and end up with a fuller understanding of the sport.

How young can you start someone sculling? Part of the answer depends on *how* you start them. In some European countries, kids are in boats well before they reach their teens. I think this is fine as long as the focus is on fun and relaxed rowing, not on competition. Important boatsmanship skills and a love of the water can both be gained by exposing kids to rowing. In terms of competing, I think the ideal age is somewhere between thirteen and sixteen, when the body is developed enough to handle the stresses to muscles and joints. Even at this age, however, I think the focus should be on skill development and fun rather than on serious competition.

How old can you start rowing? Barbara Green, who has won the Head of the Charles five times, took up sculling when she was in her late forties. Her sons had both been successful U.S. National Team scullers, and they inspired her to try the sport for herself. A few years later, she was competing against and beating women half her age. Plenty of others have taken up rowing in their retirement years, as a more vigorous alternative to tennis or golf. Naturally, you should check with your doctor if you have any serious health issues that may affect your ability to row.

ATTITUDE AND ATHLETICISM

The quality and nature of your instruction has a lot to do with the kind of person you are—and how ready you are to receive tutelage. Some scullers, for example, are virtually uncoachable. Many of these people are excellent athletes in other sports who come to rowing with a lot of preconceptions and pride. They generally need to go about things much the way I did, and get a fair number of dunkings before they sober up and start learning. Others who are unpretentious and, even, unathletic may present the coach with a much better clay to work with and mold. In the middle are the rowers who are learning largely on their own, using the coach as a person who simply confirms ideas that they already suspect are true. Remember, from a coach's standpoint, it is often the kind of enthusiasm and receptivity that you bring that determines the quality of assistance you will receive.

GENDER

Because attitude is so important in learning how to scull, a macho stance is often counterproductive. Typically, men subscribe to the brute-force method, partly because they more often rely on raw strength than many women do, and partly because they live in a culture where such displays of power are rewarded. However, applying power in a scull first requires learning grace and efficiency. Typically, women are at an advantage here, partly because of biology, and partly because they live in a culture where expressing their power has often entailed more self-restraint.

The amount of women entering the sport is increasing dramatically, and it is no longer unusual to see equal numbers of men and women showing up to receive instruction. Often, it is the women who take to the water like ducks, while men initially struggle. I frequently find myself consoling husbands, who at times get more frustrated when they see their wives doing so well. As you'll learn in the pages of this book, you need to keep your focus in your own boat and not be too concerned with how well someone else is doing. Gender aside, the point is not how talented you are initially but how dedicated you become.

WHERE TO ROW?

One of the biggest obstacles to learning how to scull is finding a place to learn and practice it properly. Many people tell me they'd like to row but there is simply no opportunity to do so where they live. They live either in a place where rowing doesn't exist or a place where rowing is inaccessible to the general public. The first obstacle is a simple matter of geography; the second is more a matter of politics. If you treat each obstacle separately, you may have better luck solving your dilemma.

In terms of the first, wherever there is a body of water big enough to row on, rowing can be done. Although classic sculling takes place on placid, slow-moving rivers, you can also boat on lakes, oceans, or estuaries. This may mean rowing in a slightly sturdier, wider craft than the finely tapered narrow shells that ply the Charles, but sometimes less traditional venues can make the sport even more fun. I spent a wonderful summer sculling in a wherry around a harbor in southern Connecticut. I raced against powerboats and surfed in their wakes, explored tidal marshes and islands—it was a real adventure.

When most people think of rowing, they assume that they have to either join a private club or have graduated from a college that has a crew program. However, many of the clubs and colleges allow for at least some public access, and very few programs will turn down someone who is a persistent, dedicated rower. One of the best resources for knowledge about rowing, in fact, is the college crew coach nearest you. Even if they can't assist you directly, they may be able to tell you where to go in terms of lessons or other rowing information.

COACHING

I'm not trying to either build up or discount the role of the coach but rather to make the point that a good instructor provides not only initial encouragement and advice but, ultimately, the means by which you can evaluate your own rowing. If you aren't improving on your own after spending a season or two with a coach, something is definitely wrong. Either you aren't making proper use of the lessons (i.e., practicing), or your instructor is somehow not getting the right information to you. Most people either blame themselves or blame their coach, but the reality usually falls somewhere in between. No matter how talented either of you may be, sometimes it's just a bad combination.

With this in mind, the best coach for you isn't necessarily the celebrated sculling pro with the gold medal around his neck. That person may be so into his own head that he can't get into yours, or his verbal skills may be rather lacking. On the other hand, you may learn a lot from that same person by simply rowing beside him silently and watching how he composes himself. In this respect, even if you don't live in a rowing mecca where you can pick and choose from *whom* you learn, you can be clever about *how* you learn.

Unlike crew coaches, sculling instructors are there to help you along your way toward a greater understanding and appreciation of the sport, not necessarily to hold your hand or provide motivation. Good scullers may not be self-taught, but they are certainly self-motivated. Chart the course of your own sculling career, and trust your instincts as to what and who can best help you get to that destination.

CAMPS

For those who scull in virtual isolation, sculling schools, such as the Craftsbury Sculling Center and the Florida Rowing Center, are often the best way for both beginning and intermediate scullers to immerse themselves in the sport for a week or weekend. Videotaped critiques, a qualified staff of both visiting and veteran coaches, and a full gamut of sculling equipment are the hallmarks of these fine programs.

One limitation of camps is that they generally provide an over-abundance of information within a very short period of time, certainly much more than the average beginner can process. Bombarded by lectures, demonstrations, and films, most campers effectively stop listening after the second day, not because they don't want to learn but because their minds and bodies are on overload. What you need as a beginner, and what a camp can't give you, is time. Time to think over the concepts and try them out on the water. Time to absorb knowledge from different sources and gradually make sense of it on your own.

EQUIPMENT

I will discuss equipment in more depth in the next chapter, but I want to underline the fact that the quality of your equipment is not directly related to the quality of your rowing. Most people mistakenly assume that a better boat will make them a better sculler. You make the boat look good, not vice versa. Likewise, buying a boat isn't like buying a car. Getting an expensive, top-of-the-line model doesn't guarantee you prestige or performance. Not only will you look and feel foolish in a boat you can't handle, but your sculling will suffer. Also, don't feel like you have to buy something right away before you educate yourself in the sport.

The author trying out a newly-built wooden boat.

CHAPTER 2

EQUIPMENT

Every change in equipment has eventually produced or even required a rethinking of technique and training.

—*Thomas Mendenhall*
A Short History of American Rowing

BOATS

In terms of their overall dimensions and external design, rowing shells have changed very little over the past century. The last big innovation came in the middle of the nineteenth century, when professional scullers in the United States, Canada, and Britain discovered the advantage of the sliding seat. Prior to that time, the rowing stroke used only the upper body from a fixed seat position. While some other innovations have been tried, such as the sliding rigger arm, they have not been accepted into this fairly conservative sport. As Thomas Mendenhall suggests, when you change the equipment too radically, you begin to change the nature of the sport itself.

What has changed, of course, are the materials and methods. For better or worse, synthetic materials have largely replaced wood, and the process of boat and oar making has become a high-tech operation rather than a one-man craft. Also, the gradual development of wider blades, which allow more "grab" at the beginning of the stroke, and the advent of various electronic devices to measure boat speed, stroke

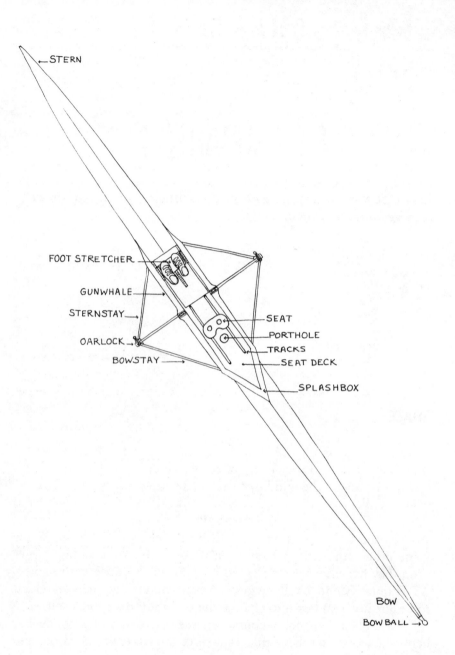

←STERN

FOOT STRETCHER

GUNWHALE

STERNSTAY

OARLOCK

BOWSTAY

SEAT

PORTHOLE

TRACKS

SEAT DECK

SPLASHBOX

BOW

BOW BALL →

rating, and the rower's heart rate have all occurred within the past decade. As in any sport, the experimentation with and development of new innovations is centered on the twin goals of speed and comfort.

Unlike in some other sports, the equipment you use for sculling matters much less than your own ability. What is more important is being in the right boat, one that matches your skill as a sculler and the conditions of the water on which you intend to do most of your rowing. Part of the emphasis of this chapter is to help you choose a boat, particularly if you are new to the sport or want to purchase a boat for the first time. The first order of business, of course, is to become familiar with the different categories of sculling boats.

CLASSES OF SCULLS

There are no classes of boats in sculling per se, and the dividing line between what is racing class and what is recreational is rather arbitrary. Roughly speaking, however, a **racing shell** is one that is over 25 feet in length and under 12 inches in beam at the widest point. Intermediate singles, sometimes known as **comps,** are between 20 and 24 feet in length and range from 13 to 20 inches in beam. Beginning boats, also known as **wherries** or **gigs,** are usually between 16 and 20 feet in length and range from 20 to 24 inches in width. Some of these latter two categories, outfitted with self-bailer units, are used in ocean rowing and racing.

If you get interested in ocean racing, you'll find that, again, few set classes exist. In such races, you pick as narrow and as light a boat as you can handle without flipping. Some river races, like the *Ernestine Bayer* race, which precedes the *Head of the Charles* every year, divide recreational rowers into various categories based on each boat's weight and length. Again, these divisions are somewhat arbitrary, and based more on what certain boat manufacturers have come up with to delineate their designs.

I'll briefly go over some of the different types of boats and their uses.

The Wonderful World of Wherries

Wherries are a wonderful way for the novice to get started in sculling. With its wide hull, a well-made wherry offers good stability, and yet it has enough roundedness to allow you to learn how to use the oars properly in balancing the boat. A decent wherry also has enough length and gradual taper toward the ends to allow the boat to **run out,** or glide nicely between strokes. This quality allows the novice to gain a sense of proper rhythm and ratio.

Unfortunately, some beginner boats have been built more with the owner's limited garage space or car rack in mind: too short, excessively flat bottomed, and without a keel to help the boat keep running straight. A poorly made wherry, or one poorly maintained, can sometimes give this class of boat a bad reputation. Many people come to the incorrect conclusion that real sculling can be experienced only in the narrowest of boats. A good wherry possesses all the attributes of any scull and affords the beginner a stable base from which to master the various nuances of technique and boat-handling.

For this reason, many rowing clubs require novices to put in a certain amount of time in a wherry before advancing to the narrower, faster boats. This policy is partly to ensure less danger to both the rower and the boat. Beginners tend to botch landings, run into bridges, capsize, and perform various other unseemly and unsafe acts. A bad landing with a wherry won't hurt the sturdy boat, whereas the same treatment of an ultralight racer could cause serious damage.

Intermediate Shells

Intermediate sculling boats, sometimes known as comps or hybrids, are the perfect starting point for you if you have some rowing experience, such as college sweep rowing, or if you want a boat to use on an ocean, estuary, or lake where the water can get rough. As I mentioned above, some of these boats come equipped with a self-draining bailer that makes rough-water rowing more enjoyable and safe. On a river, the intermediate shell is the perfect trainer for someone who has established good basic rowing skills but is not quite ready for the instability of a true racing scull.

Most comps do give you more of the feel of a racing shell while still providing greater primary stability. For this reason, the comp is an excellent boat in which to further hone your skills. *Again, the better you master technique in a stable boat, the more smoothly your skills will be transferred into a higher-level boat.*

In their eagerness to move into a better or faster boat, most people advance into less stable boats too soon. Moving up too soon usually guarantees that you'll get dusted by another rower who stayed in the wherry an extra season, perfecting his technique. Remember, the boat doesn't make you go fast, but vice versa. If you can't handle the tippier boat, you may actually go slower. If you are so busy trying to stay balanced, you won't be able to relax and use your full power on the oars.

Racing Shells

Again, the term *racing* is something of a misnomer, since all levels of boats can be and are raced. Be that as it may, these boats are used at the national and Olympic levels, and they enable the experienced sculler to attain the greatest possible speed. Racing shells are the lightest, narrowest, and most round-bottomed of shells. They are also the tippiest and the most sensitive to errors in technique. Of course, even within the designation of racing shell, there are various types of boats, and they all row somewhat differently.

In its design and construction, a racing shell expresses its manufacturer's interpretation of what makes for the fastest boat. This interpretation is, of course, somewhat subjective, and ultimately you have to make your own decision, based on your skill and the conditions of the water where you will row. What boat manufacturers hope is that good scullers will choose their boats and win races in them. Winning is the ultimate validation of their work, and one of the surest ways to ensure that they sell more boats to other scullers. The fact is, most champion scullers can win races in any decent boat, which only serves to further emphasize that it is not so much the scull but the sculler that makes the difference. Choose a boat that suits you best, not the one that someone told you was the fastest.

BUYING A BOAT

Every year I get at least a dozen phone calls from people confused about buying a boat. Some of this confusion comes from the simple fact that, unlike when you're buying a car, you can't just drive down the street and try one out at your local dealership. Shell building is still somewhat of a small business, and if you want a boat, you pretty much have to go right to the factory that makes them. Occasionally, boat manufacturers keep demos on hand to loan out to qualified scullers, but don't count on it. They usually just rely on word of mouth and the good nature of other scullers to push their products.

If you are a member of a boat club, you will come in contact with some of these boats through the club's equipment and through other members who have private singles. Before you run out and get your own boat, you should first try out as many different boats as possible. Some clubs stockpile one type of boat because of a relationship they have with a local manufacturer. This doesn't mean that you should also buy that product. Beg, rent, or borrow your way into as many boats as you can. Owning one is a rather large investment that shouldn't be entered into lightly. You don't want to end up in a boat that doesn't fit your needs. You'll just become frustrated and disenchanted with the sport.

If you row in virtual isolation, consider spending a week at a sculling camp, which offers you the chance to try out a variety of boats. Some of these actually come up for sale at the end of the season. Talk to people at regattas about their boats and ask them why they chose them. Talk to coaches. Then you can begin to make an educated choice. Buying a scull can be challenging but also very rewarding. Owning a boat of your own brings with it a commitment to the sport and a self-validation that may not be there when you are using someone else's equipment.

THE QUALITIES OF A WELL-MADE BOAT

When you begin evaluating single sculls, you should consider all of the following basic qualities of a well-made boat.

Stiffness

Stiffness generally refers to the end-to-end rigidity of the boat, from bow to stern. It is also used to refer to the torsional rigidity of the hull and the stiffness of the riggers. Both the boat and the riggers can flex when you apply power, and excessive flex means loss of power transfer to the forward motion of the shell. The easiest way to test the stiffness of the boat and riggers is to simply try to flex them. Put the boat in slings, grab hold of the rigger arms, and firmly press down. They shouldn't allow any notable flex. Now flip the boat upside down and press the stern down slowly with both hands until the bow starts to lift. Does the hull seem to give before the bow rises? You may want to perform these tests while the boat owner or manufacturer isn't looking. Most people don't like their boats poked and prodded in such a manner.

If you do have any concerns about stiffness, ask if the boat has ever been given a **deflection test,** which more accurately measures end-to-end stiffness. Basically, a dryland deflection test is done by placing the boat right side up in slings, then adding weight to the middle of the boat, where the cockpit is. A wire is stretched from the bow to the stern, and as weight is added to the cockpit area the distance from the wire down to the seat deck is measured to see how much the boat flexes. If you have any doubts about the structural integrity of your own boat, I don't recommend that you try this test on it.

Synthetic boats, especially the monocoque design (see "Synthetic Boats" in the next section), rely more on the rigidity of the outer skin to give the boat its overall stiffness. Soft-decked boats, including those made of wood, rely more on the strength of their internal framework. While there is some debate about *how much* stiffness a boat needs, stiffness in general is a desirable quality. Some of the specific differences between wood versus synthetic are dealt with below.

Weight

The common perception is that the lighter a boat is, the better it is. Boats have gotten lighter and lighter over the past several years. There is a minimum weight limit of 30.9 pounds for international racing in singles, and while many racing singles approach that number, most are in the range of 32 to 35 pounds. Decent recreational singles range from 38 to 45 pounds, fully rigged. While you obviously want your boat to be as light as possible, a few pounds aren't going to make a significant difference. In order for a boat to be comfortably carried, however, it should ideally weigh less than 40 pounds, and a competitive racing single should be under 35 pounds.

Durability

I place this quality right after weight, because in general the lighter the boat is, the less durable it is. Back in the mid–nineteenth century, when sculling was a big-money sport, singles were actually made with varnished paper skins and weighed even less than boats do today. Of course, they only lasted for one or two races, but with such good prize money it didn't matter. Today, when most people invest up to several thousand dollars in a boat, they expect it to last for a while. So they should. What many people don't realize is that some of the top synthetic racing boats—the ones you pay the most dearly for—are the ones that have the shortest shelf life. By shelf life I mean the number of years that they can maintain their optimal stiffness.

Of course, the most important factor in keeping a boat in good shape is how well you maintain it. Regardless of whether your boat is made of wood or fiberglass, you should adhere to some basic practices if you want to preserve its longevity. Keeping it out of the sun, in a dry place, and properly stored on a rack can add years to the life of your boat.

MATERIALS AND CONSTRUCTION

Wooden Shells

Traditionally, sculling boats were constructed of various woods: spruce for the keel and stringers, ash or elm for the ribs and knees, cedar or mahogany for the outer skin. Each species has its own function that contributes to the overall integrity of the shell.

To some people, wooden rowing shells are the most beautiful boats on the water and the most pleasing to row. They claim that these shells give one a feel for the water that synthetics simply cannot. In terms of racing performance, a lightweight, well-made wooden single is not a disadvantage, despite the common misconception that wooden boats are slow. It is certainly more difficult to produce a stiff wood boat that is also light in weight, but in the single-scull class it is entirely possible. One problem is that there just aren't that many good wooden boatbuilders left. The other is that consumer demand just isn't there.

With the advent of synthetics, the wooden shell has taken a back seat in the hearts and minds of the general public. Nevertheless, the more you understand about the amazing attributes of wood, the more you may want to consider owning or perhaps even building one. If taken care of, a wooden shell can hold its stiffness at least as long as its synthetic counterpart, in part because the natural flex of a wooden shell allows it to spring back into shape, instead of snapping at the glue line. Most of the horror stories—the warping and the rotting—are due to poorly maintained boats. You have to keep a wooden boat varnished and watertight, and many people simply don't have the time or patience for this maintenance.

Synthetic Boats

The first synthetic sculls came on the scene in the 1970s, although fiberglass, Kevlar, and carbon fiber had already been in use for some time in the boating and aerospace industries. The first fiberglass shells were not all that pretty. Some had ripples or puckers in the hull, and others were in fact quite heavy. In the past twenty years, however, the art of synthetic boatbuilding has advanced rapidly, to the point that most of what you see is handsome and well-made.

Many plastic boat owners don't know exactly what synthetic boat making is all about. Terms like *Kevlar, carbon,* and *monocoque* are batted about by the boat manufacturers but not really understood by the buying public. While you may not care what your boat is made of, or how it is made, knowing a little about the materials and construction may help you decide what to own. Furthermore, this knowledge may help you better understand how to maintain and preserve the longevity of your shell.

The first synthetic boats were actually hybrids, made of the same wooden framework as wooden shells but having abandoned the outer cedar or mahogany skin in favor of fiberglass. This offered an interesting combination of a more durable hull material wrapped around the classic skeletal framework of a wooden shell. Some boat makers still offer this type of hybrid for those rowers who favor the feel of a wooden frame and gunwales. Most, however, went on to experiment with eliminating wooden frames altogether, either by replacing them with synthetic materials or dispensing with the need for framing entirely. **Carbon fiber,** light in weight and very strong, began to be substituted for wood in the keels and the knees, and subsequently appeared more and more in the overall hull material of the boat.

Most top-of-the-line shells are **monocoque** design boats with a **cored-skin construction,** either honeycomb or foam. The honeycomb or the foam is sandwiched in between an outer and inner layer of fiberglass, carbon, or Kevlar, and provides the hull with extra rigidity and strength while keeping the overall weight of the boat relatively light. This strength in the outer hull omits the necessity of the classic internal framework. Naturally, the whole sandwich is only as strong as the glue that holds it all together, and the epoxy or polyester resins used for these boats can break down if they aren't maintained properly. Left out in the sun or stored in a damp place, a synthetic boat will suffer just as much degradation as a wooden one. Excessive use or abuse by irresponsible club scullers will also cause a composite boat to become prematurely soft, not to mention the numerous dings and dents due to small collisions with docks, logs, and other boats.

Single-skin boats, made with layered cloth of **Kevlar** or **fiberglass,** are generally more durable than their cored cousins but not as light in weight given equal stiffness. They are also a little easier to repair if they get damaged, because you don't have to deal with filling in or replacing the core material; you only have to patch the skin. The other synthetic material, already mentioned, that can offer a boat rigidity and durability while remaining lightweight is carbon fiber. It is fairly expensive and it does have one physical drawback: used by itself, carbon fiber doesn't have great impact resistance, the kind you need to withstand the occasional log or rock that may come in contact with your hull. If and when it breaks, carbon fiber is harder to repair than either fiberglass or Kevlar. Most synthetic boat manufacturers use some combination of fiberglass, Kevlar, and carbon to try to combine stiffness, lightness, and durability.

What you have to remember when shopping for a synthetic boat is that, in comparison to wood, they haven't been around all that long. There is still much learning and experimenting to be done with these and other materials. So be patient and ask questions until you find the boat you'll be happy owning.

OARS

As with boats, oars—or **sculls**—were once made entirely of wood. While there are a few reactionary scullers like myself left who still row with wooden oars, almost everyone now uses carbon-fiber sculls. They are generally a lot easier to maintain, offer adjustable features, and sport the radical new blade shapes that have captured the attention of the new generation of rowers.

Stiffness and Weight

As with boats, there are a few basic things to look for when you purchase oars. Stiffness, again, is a desirable feature. You can lean a set of oars against a wall and flex them to compare the relative stiffness of one set against another. Lightness is generally a plus, especially if you are going to row distances of any substantial length. You have to be a little careful in assessing weight, however. The overall weight of an oar is sometimes less important than its weight resting in the oarlock.

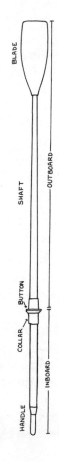

Construction and Durability

Fine wooden oars are generally made of several layers of Sitka spruce, laminated together and left hollow in the middle. A thin layer of ash is sometimes incorporated onto the flat part of the shaft and on the tip of the blade for extra strength and durability. Fine synthetic oars are made of wound carbon fiber, hollow throughout the shaft. Despite the reputation of carbon for shattering when hit hard, the construction of these carbon oars has proven to be excellent. They will break if you hit something like a bridge with enough force, but so will a wooden oar. Besides, it's better for the oar to break than for it to transfer the force of impact to the boat or to you.

For club programs whose equipment gets a lot of use, aluminum oars are a wonderful and inexpensive option.

Adjustability

Newer oars offer numerous features that allow you to play with different blade shapes, overall length, and grip size. For rigging fanatics and coaches, these features are lots of fun. For the general public, they can be a little confusing and frustrating. Also, as I'll talk about in the chapter on rigging, anything adjustable can fall out of adjustment. Keep this in mind when you decide to make a purchase. Unless you plan to do a lot of experimenting, or to row in team boats, a fixed oar probably makes more sense.

Blade Shape

The big change in oars since the 1980s has been the blade shape. The symmetrical **macon blade** has been largely abandoned in favor of the wider **hatchet** style, which is mounted on a shorter shaft to compensate for the added load. This asymmetrical, wider blade is actually a new take on an old technology, first invented by professional sculler and rigger Michael Davis in the 1870s and known then as the "leg of mutton" design. Hatchet oars allow for a more vertical carriage of the oar through the water and provide an unquestionable speed advantage in sweep rowing.

In sculling, which is a much more efficient motion to begin with, the benefit of hatchets is not so clear cut. A well-known American oar maker confessed to me that in numerous tests given to his own nationally ranked sons, no noticeable speed loss or gain was evident. For those who learn to scull well with traditional blades, hatchets may offer little inherent advantage. However, as with the big-head tennis rackets that came out in the 1970s, bigger blades do make it easier for the less skilled practitioner to connect solidly with the water and thereby relax and pull hard with more confidence. This fact in itself will probably cause the extinction of the macon blade. Those who begin their sculling careers with hatchets are unlikely to switch back to the more difficult macon.

When I first teach students how to scull, I stick to the old-style macon blades, which require beginners to develop the finesse that will serve them well throughout their sculling careers. Once they have become accomplished and wish to compete, I encourage them to experiment with hatchets and/or different length oars, in search of speed and comfort. While many find the hatchets useful, others object to the added back strain they can cause and claim the blade shape has no effect on their times.

Just for the record, I use a pair of custom-made wooden oars with macon blades that are nearly as light as anything else out there and have a feel for the water that, in my own mind, is unmatched by anything synthetic. Again, as with boat selection, the ultimate test for a set of sculls is to try them on the water.

ELECTRONIC MEASURING DEVICES

If you plan on eventually doing some racing, you will find that electronic devices can be very useful tools in establishing what works best for you in terms of equipment, rigging, and technique. It is much better, of course, to have a coach monitoring all these details while you simply focus on the business of rowing well. But many scullers don't have this luxury.

Speed and Rate Meters

For many years, rowers and coaches made due with nothing more than a watch or a **strokewatch**, a simple, stopwatchlike tool used to calculate the number of strokes per minute. By checking the strokewatch and watching the spacing of the puddles made by the oars, a good coach could get a rough idea of boat speed. For scullers, doing set pieces between bridges or marks on the river while experimenting with different rigs and ratings (i.e., number of strokes per minute) has always been the ultimate test of speed. The advent of the propeller-driven **speed coach,** which gives second-by-second readouts of speed and stroke rating, has made some of this analysis a bit faster and easier. Naturally, you always have to take into account the varying water and wind conditions as you execute your tests.

Another nifty feature of the speed coach is that you can program in custom workouts and even replay and store the information of a given piece. In this sense the newer units have become like small computers. After you've done your tests and found your rig, however, I suggest you turn the little box off and tune in to the workings of your own body. One of the dangers of the speed coach, I believe, is that it turns the rowing shell into an ergometer. In trying to attain higher and higher speeds, you may focus on pulling harder rather than smoothing out your technique.

Heart-Rate Monitors

A heart-rate monitor is an excellent way to gauge how hard you are working your heart. The device straps around your chest and sends a wireless signal either to a wristwatch or directly into some speed-coach units. Many people have little idea of the cardiovascular intensity of their workouts, and some initial time spent with this device can be very useful in developing optimal workouts and racing strategies. You may have the tendency to go over the edge in terms of your fitness ability, and not pace yourself wisely. Or you may not know how hard to push. By making some correlations between heart rate and stroke rate, you may be able to better regulate your efforts (see chapter 7 for details on training with a monitor). Of course, you can also take your pulse manually, with a stopwatch, but it isn't as accurate and you have to stop rowing.

GPS (Global Positioning System)

For those who venture onto a large body of water, whether it is a lake or an ocean, a GPS unit is not only useful but can be a lifesaver.

By taking readings from orbiting satellites, these portable electronic devices provide the rower with the steering sense of a homing pigeon. Simply plot in your intended course, and the little unit directs you along, telling you when you're veering off course. For ocean-racing enthusiasts, as well as for those who don't want to get lost in the fog, a GPS unit is worth the investment.

Instructor, Kate Matwychuck, working with a novice in the sculling tank.

CHAPTER 3

TECHNIQUE

If rowing can be made to seem easy, it will be easy.

—*Steve Fairbairn, famous Australian rowing coach*

What is technique and why do you need it? While these questions may seem rather foolish, they lie at the heart of understanding the relevance of all those skill-building drills you may inevitably be asked to suffer. They are also, quite frankly, the queries that lie largely unspoken on the lips of almost every sculler. If you are a coach and you can't adequately answer these questions, you have no reason to expect your charges to follow your direction. After all, how difficult can the sculling motion be? Why waste time on boring exercises and theory instead of just enjoying the natural, fluid motion?

Indeed, at least a few boat manufacturers espouse the belief that an initial ten-minute lesson is adequate for most people to be on their way. The rest will come through self-practice and intuition. Plenty of potential buyers are willing to believe this. You can usually spot these people on the water or in a health club, looking a little rough perhaps, but nevertheless enjoying themselves in a training shell or on a rowing machine. To those of us with some expertise in rowing, what these folks are doing may seem disturbing and aesthetically incorrect, and our immediate instinct is to correct or refine the motion. But who is to say, really, what proper technique is?

The basic elements of the sculling stroke *are* fairly well defined by the equipment: the sliding seat, the dimensions of the boat, and the oars. Therefore, you would think that if you put a group of novice scullers into rowing shells and provided them with very basic instruction, eventually they would figure out naturally the best way to use sculls. While this hypothesis is attractive, one of the fundamental problems with it is that sculling is *not* a natural motion, despite what it may look like from afar when performed by good scullers. Within the deceptive framework of those smooth strokes lies a studied and very subtle set of complex movements. Without the help of a knowledgeable coach or experienced sculler-mentor, you would need to have substantial knowledge of physics and human physiology to be able to figure out an efficient, natural stroke. Or just be damn lucky.

TECHNIQUE VS. STYLE

One other problem with the "learn naturally" hypothesis is that the sculling motion, as simple and as restricted as it looks, leaves plenty of room for individual interpretation. Thus, left alone for a while, our group of guinea pig novice scullers would probably all exhibit slightly different ways of rowing. Which one would be correct? Given an equal level of fitness, the sculler who could move her boat farther faster would have figured out the best way to row. So what is technique and why do you need it? *Technique, simply stated, is the most efficient way for you to move your boat across the water.* That's it.

What this definition acknowledges is that every individual sculler will eventually develop his or her own style, or interpretation of basic technique. It doesn't mean, however, that you should forgo the initial process of learning the basics through the help of a coach or another sculler. Once you have learned enough to be able to analyze your own stroke and to compare it to others, you can begin to experiment with some ideas of your own.

Like beginning artists, many novices try to copy the style of other scullers they observe—especially those who are winning big races. Important lessons can be learned through such imitation, but keep in mind that every sculler will scull somewhat differently, depending on what his or her body can do. Don't fret if you don't row exactly the same way as the next big sculler to rise to the top. Just make sure the basics of your stroke are kept intact, and your own style will develop quite naturally on its own.

Developing a good stroke is both a science and an art, a conscientious study of stroke mechanics and an effort to translate these ideas through your body and your boat. The two processes need not be at odds with each other. If you are like most scullers, throughout your first few years of development you will jump back and forth between analysis and synthesis, theory and practice, technique and style.

BASIC STROKE MECHANICS AND TERMINOLOGY

Ideally, the **stroke cycle** is a continuous, fluid motion, with no real beginning or endpoint. In order to understand and analyze the rowing motion, however, labeling and discussing its different components is helpful. Classically, the stroke is divided into two parts, the **drive** and the **recovery**. The drive, literally, is when the oars are being driven through the water by the force of your body upon them, propelling the boat. The recovery is when the oars are out of the water, being readied for the next stroke.

The beginning of the drive, when the oars contact the water, is known as the **catch.** The end of the drive, where the oars come out of the water, is commonly known as the **finish,** or release. As you progress in sculling you will come to understand these two points less as starting and end points for the drive and more as transition areas that link the drive and the recovery. Likewise, you will come to learn that it is the fluidity of the catch and the finish, or how smoothly the oars engage and disengage from the water, that marks your skill as a sculler.

Naturally, during the drive the objective is to apply force to the oars in a manner that is not only powerful but efficient. During the recovery, the objective is to exit smoothly from the water and ready the blades and the body as gracefully as possible, so as not to disturb the continued glide of the shell. Herein lies one of the elemental challenges in the art of sculling: how to balance power with grace.

BODY MOTION

The foundation of good rowing begins with an understanding of the basic body movements used to execute a stroke. Before you get too caught up in the more complex tasks of holding and feathering the

THE USE OF ERGOMETERS AND ROWING MACHINES

Some coaches argue that it is better to learn how to scull in a real boat from day one, and that rowing machines are not only a waste of time but actually detrimental to the development of good sculling technique. They have a valid point. No rowing machine can reproduce the conditions of real rowing. At best, ergs provide rowers with a decent way to keep in shape during the winter and give coaches a general indication of each athlete's fitness level. They do not, unfortunately, teach you much about finesse, both in terms of bladework and in regard to those extraneous body movements that may upset the balance and the glide of the shell.

With this in mind, I suggest you spend as many of your days on the water as possible. Still, as an initial training device, and for those without access to a boat, an ergometer can prove a useful tool. For those interested in competing, ergs are also very helpful in establishing just how hard you can push yourself. Free from the technical constraints and distractions of the water, erg training can give you a glimpse at your ultimate physiological potential.

oars or how to balance a boat, you should make sure that you know how to efficiently generate power and travel back and forth smoothly on a sliding seat. If you have access to a decent rowing machine or a rowing tank, I suggest that you begin your first efforts here, on dry land. Within a few minutes, especially with the aid of a mirror and/or a coach, you can establish the rather simple but important sequencing between the legs, the back, and the arms.

Beginning at the Finish: The Recovery Sequence

While practicing on the water, most crews and scullers tend to begin the stroke from the finish position, where the legs are laid flat and the oar handles are drawn into the waist (see fig. 1). The blades are feathered, and lie flat on the water to help balance the boat at a dead stop. From here the arms extend forward, over the knees, and then the back is bent forward, pivoting from the hips. Bend forward only as much as your flexibility allows; i.e., don't slouch or hunch over your oars (see figs. 2 and 3).

The upper body is now set and can be drawn forward by relaxing the hamstring muscles and allowing the knees to bend. As much as possible, try not to pull yourself forward by drawing against the footstretchers, or shoes. This will stop or check the glide of a shell. As you gently slide forward, control your approach to the catch with your hamstrings and keep your upper body poised but relaxed and your arms straight. Also be careful to maintain the established angle between your hip and shoulder (i.e., don't straighten up or hunch over) (see figs. 3 and 4). It is during this controlled movement of the body toward the stern that the oar blades are also being rolled into the squared position (see "Squaring" on page 39).

The Drive Sequence

When you reach the catch position (see fig. 5), where the blades are squared and just set into the water, push off the footboard without hesitation. This begins the drive portion of the stroke. As you push with the legs, feel the resistance in your back and lats, but don't start

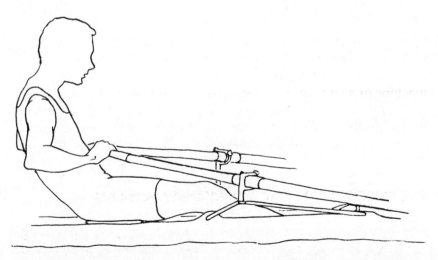

Fig. 1

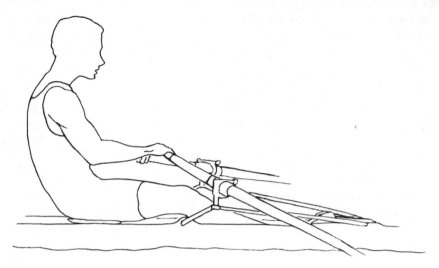

Fig. 2

to swing out of the locked tuck position with your back until your legs are nearly flat. Let the legs do the lion's share of the work in setting the boat in motion, then follow through with the back and the arms. This doesn't mean that you should disengage the upper body from the leg drive and abandon your upper-body posture; it just means that the leg

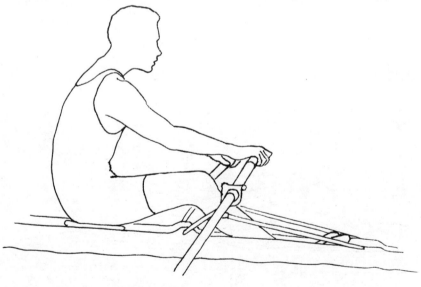

Fig. 3

Fig. 4

power takes precedence. The back should start to swing just before the legs come to rest, and the forearms begin to pull just before the back has come to rest. In this relaylike way, the three muscle groups are used to carry the oars through the water at a constant speed. Developing a smooth sense of linking the legs, back, and arms together is an essential first step to sculling well. (See figs. 6, 7, and 8.)

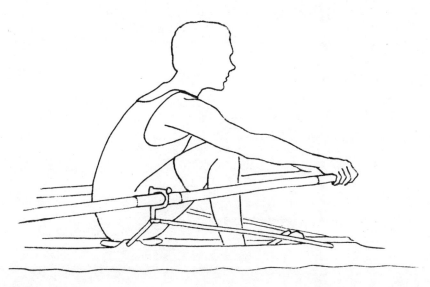

Fig. 5

Technique

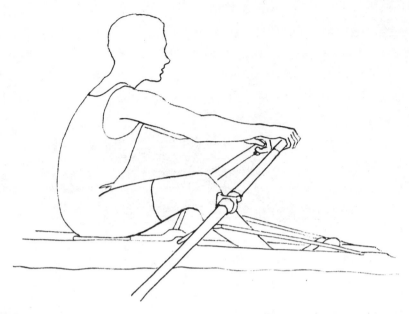

Fig. 6

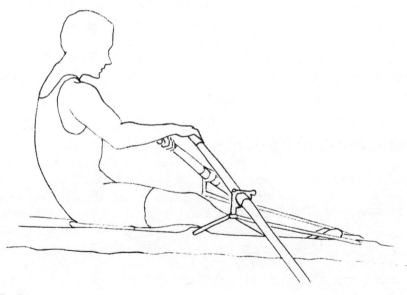

Fig. 7

Essential Sculling

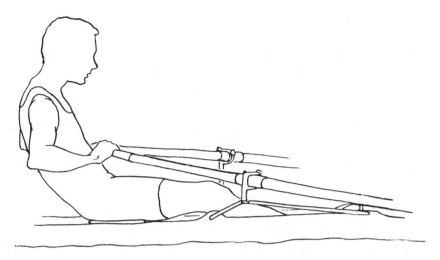

Fig. 8

Slide Control and Ratio

As I mentioned before, once you master the sequencing of the drive and the recovery cycles, you want to blend them together so that your strokes are done in a fluid, seamless fashion. It is important, however, to keep the drive and the recovery distinct in terms of their relative speed. While the drive can be done as fast and as hard as you like, the recovery should be relatively controlled to allow adequate preparation for the next catch. The classic advice for training is to maintain a **one-to-two speed ratio** between the drive and the recovery. I'll say a little more about why this is so when I talk about run, or the forward glide of the boat.

BLADE AND HAND MOTION

While you ultimately want to think of your oars as an extension of your body, obeying your every command, you weren't born with them strapped to your hands. It will take some time to synchronize your body movements and the movement of your blades, especially given the fact that you can't very easily look at your oars as you row. Aside from being an aesthetic faux pas, studying your blades is a sure way to invite capsize or collision.

Blade Depth and Hand Levels

The first thing I like to point out to beginners is how shallow the blades should be as they travel through the water on the drive. If you let your blades rest in the water in a squared or vertical position, they should float at the desired location, just below the surface. Likewise, as you begin to row, the course your hands and oar handles will take during the pull-through is prescribed by the blade itself—what it requires to stay just buried in the water. Unlike rowboat oars, which are driven deep into the water as the rower makes a wide, circular motion with the hands, sculls are drawn along relatively level.

No extra effort or muscling should be required to hold the blade in the water. If you grip the oar handles too tightly or throw your upper body into the catch, you may end up driving the blade down deeper than is necessary, wasting effort and possibly preventing a smooth exit from the water. Other blade-depth problems may occur if the blade does not enter the water at the correct catch angle. A properly rigged boat will provide this slight (4- to 7-degree) inclination of the blade, built into the oar or oarlock, which helps keep the blade from either diving down or surfing out of its placement just below the surface—the result of an **undersquared** or **oversquared** blade. I'll discuss what to do if this part of the rigging is off in chapter 8.

On the recovery, the blade is rotated into its feathered, or horizontal, position and held just above the water's surface to reduce the drag caused by wind or waves. In order to keep the blade from touching the water, the oar handles must be held on a slightly lower plane than the one your hands traced on the drive, but the plane should also be flat and level. Again, for those of you with rowboating backgrounds, there is no need to push the oar handles down all the way to the boat's gunwales. In fact, scooping down like this will hamper a decent stroke.

If you have the benefit of a stable boat or a tank to practice in, you can spend some time watching your blades to make sure they are following the right path in and out of the water. When you are confident that they are moving well, you should focus on translating blade levels to oar-handle levels and gaining a sense of where your blades are in the water on the drive and the recovery without needing to look at them. Every once in a while, even when you become proficient, take the time to make sure you are not "skying" your blades on the recovery (lifting them too high off the water) or digging too deep on the drive, thereby creating more work for yourself.

Feathering

As your blades come out of the water at the end of the drive, they are feathered, or rotated into a horizontal position. Once again, the oarlocks possess a flat, horizontal portion, a sill, which will hold the oars nicely in their correct position if your hands are sufficiently relaxed. Unlike the gradual process of "squaring" the blade, feathering needs to happen rather quickly because of the speed at which the oars are traveling through the water. *Still, you want to make sure that you push the oar handles down, lifting the blade out of the water, before you start feathering the blade.* Feathering was invented not to extract the blades from the water but to allow for less wind and water resistance on the blade during the recovery. You can, in fact, row without a feather to your stroke, and it is an excellent drill to master.

After a bit of practice, the pushing down and subsequent feathering of the oar handles will become one integrated motion, but in the beginning, it is important to make sure to get the right sequence. If you feather the

THE USE OF TANKS, BARGES, AND DOUBLES

If you are fortunate enough to have access to a sculling tank, barge, or double scull, you can study your oars, and by all means, you should. Having a stable, stationary platform from which to experiment with the basic sculling motion is invaluable in translating the ideal visual pattern of the blades into a tactile one. Here you can see exactly what happens when you raise or lower your hands during the recovery, for example, instead of relying on a coach to tell you that your blades are too high or too low to the water.

Rowing in a double scull, especially with an experienced sculler, can be even more valuable. By sitting with his blades flat on the water, the experienced sculler can create a stable platform from which you can execute your first strokes. If you have some experience, you can sit in the bow and alternate rowing with your partner. Watching that person's blades and body motion and feeling the run of the boat will greatly accelerate your progress. If you have very little experience you may want to sit in the stern, so that your veteran partner can take care of steering.

blades while they are still under the water, you'll find that they don't come out cleanly. In getting a clean, comfortable feathering motion, the other thing you want to experiment with is the position of your elbows just before you feather. Some scullers try to pull their elbows in tight to the body at the finish of the stroke, which makes it more difficult to feather correctly. Instead, as you close off the stroke, try keeping your elbows on the same horizontal plane as the hands. Let them swing up and away from the body. Doing this allows a straighter line from elbow to hand, a more relaxed forearm and grip.

FEATHERING TIPS

To feather correctly, relax your grip on the oar and let your hand open up. Most beginners try to feather the blade by gripping the oar handle and rotating the whole hand. Not only will this create technical problems later in the stroke but it is also very uncomfortable and can cause tendinitis. Instead, using your fingertips and thumb for leverage, roll the oar handle away from you in much the same motion you would use if you were trying to singlehandedly wipe some stray peanut butter off of your palm. If you're not a sloppy peanut butter eater, take a thick dowel or a can and practice rolling it around on a tabletop for a while, until you can let your fingers open and close without bending your wrist.

(continued)

Crossover

For all its symmetry and beauty, sculling does possess one odd technical hitch: the crossover of the oar handles through the middle of the stroke. In my mind, this is one of the more neglected areas of concern, particularly for beginners. Many novices struggle their way through this stage and occasionally develop an improper delivery of the hands that can hamper the flow of their stroke around the finish.

As a novice, you may wonder: why do oar handles have to cross over anyway? After all, rowboats don't require such fuss. The reason is partly provided by Archimedes, who claimed that if he had a long enough lever he could move the earth. While most of us don't have such high aspirations for our rowing, the increased leverage offered by letting the oar handles cross over is worth the added technical challenge. The answer is also partly due to the fact that most rowboats don't have sliding seats, which dramatically increases the length of the stroke (not to mention the speed of the boat). If you didn't have crossover in a racing shell you would be hard pressed to keep your hands on the oars at the catch, unless you had incredibly long arms. You would also have to draw them rather uncomfortably past your waist to complete the stroke. Try going back to a rowboat after you've learned how to scull. You'll feel quite put out.

Like many other novice scullers, I was simply told to row with my left hand stacked on top of my right. That's it. No further elaboration. If you were also given the advice "Don't break the arms early," you could easily arrive at the conclusion that the hands should be stacked directly on top of each other when they cross, a technique that generally leads to bloody knuckles. Why? The rigging of most singles is such that the starboard, or right, oarlock is only about a half inch higher than the port, and this height difference really isn't enough to allow you to stack the oar handles and keep the boat level. In most boats, if the gunwales are level, the handles will practically be touching each other, the bottom of the left to the top of the right. There isn't enough space to fit a hand in between them—unless it wants to get scraped!

A better solution is to hold the starboard oar a little farther away from you on the horizontal plane (see fig. 9). When you apply this to the recovery, it will mean leading away from the body with the left hand first, and then slipping or

While you are playing with your cylinder of choice, notice a few things. First, you need a certain amount of downward pressure against the dowel or can to make it roll in and out along the underside of your fingers. In a boat this is provided by the weight of the blades suspended over the water. The corresponding upward pressure of the oar handles against your palms is virtually all you need to hold on to the oars during the recovery. To de-emphasize the tight grip that most scullers employ, some coaches have their scullers practice rowing with the fingers completely extended on the recovery. Naturally, this is difficult to practice when the water is rough, but it is a worthwhile drill for those who tend to "death-grip" the oars.

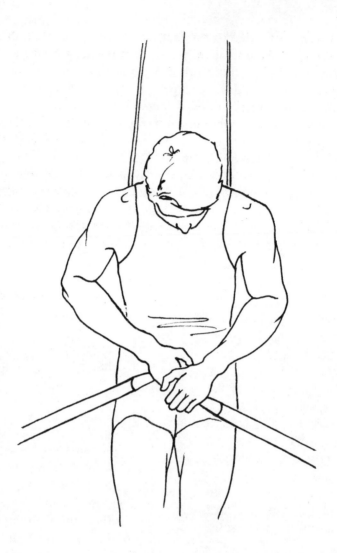

Fig. 9

nestling the right hand in just behind it. After the crossover, when the
hands swing free of each other, the right hand can catch up and enter
the water at the same angle as the left. On the drive, the oar handles
should achieve this same relationship; in this case you'll draw the
right hand in slightly before the left. There are two ways to accomplish this. One is simply to start breaking the right arm sooner; the
other (and the better, I believe) is to let your back twist a little so that
your left shoulder is canted a little farther forward toward the stern,
which effectively lengthens the left arm at this point of the stroke.

Essential Sculling

Naturally, the obvious question presents itself: why can't you just change your rigging to allow for less crossover and/or more height spacing between the two oarlocks? You can, of course, but you'll have less leverage (thus more load) by decreasing the inboard (see chapter 8, "Rigging"). The unequal oarlock heights are less of an issue, but most shells allow for only about an inch difference without bothersome meddling to the rig. I do make these allowances, however, particularly for novices who can't handle such tight tolerances. On the other side of the spectrum, open-water rowers sometimes rig their oarlocks with no height difference and allow their hands to cross over in whatever position the waves dictate (sometimes left over right, sometimes right over left).

Squaring

If you have a relaxed grip and an oar handle of the right size, you should be able to cradle the handle in your fingers and not in your palm during the recovery. As you approach the catch, squaring the blade, or "rolling up," is easily accomplished by curling the fingers back into a relaxed fist. This should be done smoothly and gradually, beginning sometime after your arms pass over your knees.

Exactly when you should begin to square the blade is a point of style. Some say an early roll-up exposes the blade to potential ill effects of the wind (and the waves), but a late roll-up often prevents a relaxed, solid catch. Having watched films of the great Russian sculler Vyasheslav Ivanov, who barely feathered his blades at all, my general take on the matter is that proper blade preparation takes precedence. If your blade isn't fully squared before the catch, you can't relax your grip and let it fall into the water.

Taking the Catch

The catch is where the blades enter the water and begin the pull-through, or drive. If you've been practicing on a rowing machine, you may tend to think of the catch as the beginning of the drive, where power is applied to the oars via the legs and back. When you think about the catch in terms of blade motion, however, it helps to consider it more as the last part of the recovery. The blade shouldn't hesitate or hang above the water until you are ready to push off the footboard. Doing this will cause you to miss water or "row into the stroke."

Instead, a split second before you push with your legs, the blade should already be entering the water. In a sense, the forward or upward release of the blades to the water and the downward depression of the legs should operate in the same way you operate the clutch and the gas pedal on a stick-shift car. (If you drive an automatic, you're out of luck with this analogy.) The oars are functioning like the clutch, lifting to engage the moving "gears" of the water, and your legs are almost simultaneously applying the gas. Those who have driven a stick know what happens when you don't time the two just right. The car stalls out if you don't give it gas, and jerks if you hesitate in lifting the clutch.

If you don't drive a stick shift, just keep in mind that in terms of your body, the catch is where you are pushing off the footboard to initiate the drive. Before this happens, of course, you have to make sure that your blades are solidly anchored in the water, and not still hovering above it. However, this is just what happens to most beginning scullers, sometimes because of the late squaring practice mentioned above, and sometimes because of a lack of body preparation, or correct posture, at the catch.

BOAT MOTION

While you are working on the efficiency of your body motion and your bladework skills, you will face the additional challenge of keeping your boat balanced and running smoothly through the water. Rowing machines and tanks are good practice for body-motion and bladework skills, but rowing in a shell is essential for boat-motion skills.

Balancing a Boat at Rest

When you first sit down in a single scull, you will immediately feel how tippy it is compared to other boats. Unlike a rowboat or even a kayak, it has very little stability to offer. This is due not only to its narrow dimensions and the roundness of the hull but to the relatively high center of gravity of the sliding seat. Without the use of the oars for balance, most rowing shells will quickly capsize.

When the scull is not in motion, the oars must be flat on the water to assist with balance. In this resting position, the oars serve as pontoons or outriggers, and by holding the oar handles in your hands or cradling them in your lap, you can relax and get your bearings without being too concerned about flipping. This position is also an excellent way to ride out a large wake from a passing powerboat.

If you move your oar handles up and down, in opposite directions to each other, the boat will pitch to port and starboard. By playing with the oar handles like this, you will quickly discover how a rowing shell is balanced by oar-handle levels and not with the body. Subtle shifts of body weight and tension will occur quite naturally, but you should not purposefully lean to try to balance the boat. Always keep yourself centered directly over the keel.

Balancing a Boat in Motion

When a scull is set in motion, the oar blades can be held above the water and the boat will stay on keel by virtue of its forward momentum. Balancing like this is possible for the same reason that you could take your hands off the handlebars of your moving bicycle as a kid. As you may remember, to keep the bike from swerving you had to be very careful not to shift your body weight around. This initially meant keeping very still while coasting, or later on learning to pedal with a very constant, smooth motion that would not cause the frame or the handlebars to shimmy.

Some of the same principles hold true in sculling. If your oars come out of the water cleanly at the finish, and you keep your body weight over the keel, your boat should balance on the hull alone. Some coaches let novices drag or skim their blades on the water during the recovery to assist with balance, but this habit will only hamper the development of good technique. If you can't get your blades off the water despite constant practice, chances are that you need to move into a more stable boat for a while.

Run, Ratio, and Rhythm

Good balance is a prerequisite for **run,** the glide of the boat that you want to maintain between strokes. Naturally, if you can't get your blades off the water, they'll slow down your glide considerably. The

PAUSE DRILLS

Developing a sensitivity to your hands, as they control the oars during the recovery, and to your body weight, as it moves forward from the finish position, takes time and patience. To better calibrate the hands and the body, the following "pause drills" are often practiced.

Pause at the Finish

Taking one stroke at a time, stop rowing right after you push down and feather the blades out of the water. Let the boat glide while you continue to hold your blades a few inches above the water's surface. Concentrate on getting a clean exit from the water with both oars, and if your balance falters, use your hands to make small shifts to the oar-handle levels. Should one of your blades get stuck to the water, gently rotate the oar handle away from you slightly (as if you were about to square) to release it from the surface tension.

Pause over the Knees

Finish the stroke and let the arms extend over the knees, *(continued)*

other, more subtle factor in achieving run has to do with how smoothly you can negotiate your body weight back and forth along the slide, particularly on the recovery. I've already mentioned **slide control** in talking about basic body motion, but it starts to make sense only when you're in a boat.

Again, try to maintain a two-to-one ratio of recovery speed to drive, and keep in mind that what you are doing when your oars are out of the water is as important as what you are doing when they are in. After you have taken a stroke and your boat is gliding forward, you ideally want to maintain that glide as you come forward to take your next stroke. If you rush into the stern, then stop abruptly before the catch, the boat will check, or slow down. Of course, every rower does this to a greater or lesser extent, and it is very instructive to watch how well each crew or individual can maintain boat speed between strokes.

Novices tend to be too focused on pulling as hard as possible on the drive and getting to the next stroke as quickly as possible during the recovery. The boat lunges forward eagerly but stalls out just as quickly. Experienced crews pausing here instead of in your lap. Don't let your shoulders come out of the bow; only the hands move away. Most people find this to be the easiest pause drill, which isn't surprising: the oars are directly perpendicular to the boat here, and this greatly assists balance.

Body-Over Pause

Instead of stopping to pause over the knees, let the upper body pivot forward from the waist, so that your oar handles are now a bit farther into the stern. You should ideally bend forward here to what will be your set body angle for the catch. This way you won't have to lunge forward at the last second to get extra reach. In reality, however, different people have different degrees of back flexibility, and some may not be able to bend very far forward with their legs still laid flat. If you are one of these people, don't hunch over or get into an uncomfortable body-over position in an effort to get more reach. Instead, try to work on your lower-back flexibility and strength before and after you row.

and scullers can make their boats move smoothly through the water at a more constant speed, by controlling the speed of slides on the recovery and by negotiating body weight in a nondisruptive way.

If you watch veteran scullers, try to determine where they seem to pause or gather for their next stroke. As I mentioned earlier, most scullers have a point somewhere in the recovery where they break this fluid motion of the stroke cycle. This point often corresponds to one of the pause drills (see page 42). This point usually has to do with a particular rowing style or the particular build of the rower. In any case, this interpretation of the stroke cycle becomes part of the **rhythm.** Heavyweight scullers, for example, often row with a pronounced pause at the waist, employing a long drive and layback position. Lightweights, who have less to offer in power but perhaps more in endurance, often develop a quick finish and deft exit from the bow. I'll talk more about some of the other factors concerning technique and style in chapter 6, "Structure and Flow."

Sculling instructor Jamie Walen demonstrating how to balance a boat with a rather unorthodox drill.

CHAPTER 4

BOAT-HANDLING SKILLS

There is nothing—absolutely nothing—half so much worth doing as simply messing about in boats.

—*Kenneth Grahame,* The Wind in the Willows

In addition to learning stroke technique, you should master several boat-handling skills to preserve your equipment and make your outings more enjoyable. Most of these look deceptively simple, but each of them requires an initial amount of study and practice if you want to execute them well. Perfect these skills so that you can have them at your disposal and you'll be more confident.

CARRYING A SHELL

There are different ways to carry boats, depending on their design and construction. When you are selecting a carrying method, keep three things in mind. First, make sure that you have a good enough hold on the boat so that you won't drop it if a strong wind comes along. Second, make sure that the carry is relatively comfortable and doesn't strain your neck or back. Third, make sure that the boat itself is not being stressed. The methods below are mainly for use with intermediate and advanced shells that are no wider than 18 inches and weigh less than 40 pounds. If your boat is bigger than this, read the section entitled "Carrying Bigger Boats."

The gunwales and the hull of most fine racing shells are generally not good places to grab; they may crack or even break. The riggers are a better choice but should be used sparingly, for they were not designed to support the entire weight of the boat. The seat-deck area, which has been designed to hold your weight as you row, is the best location for handholds. Most boats have either portals or handles at either end, where the seat tracks begin and end. If your boat is well built, its center of gravity will lie somewhere between these two points, allowing you to balance it rather nicely at your waist. If you don't have far to go and your boat is on the heavy side of 40 pounds, you can lift and carry it right side up.

Getting It Off a Boat Rack

Most shells are stored upside down on a boat rack, which allows any water inside to drain out freely. Getting a shell off a rack requires a little finesse, especially when it is packed in tightly among a group of others. If it is stored below waist level or on the ground, you will unfortunately have to grab the riggers or the gunwales to lift the boat and roll it right side up. If you have a set of slings, you can use them to support the shell as you roll it. If not, balance the hull on your knee while you switch your grips to the inside of the boat.

If your boat is stored at waist level or higher, things are a little easier. Simply reach in and grab the two handholds. Rest the palms of your hands on the seat deck as you do this, and keep your fingers wrapped around the handles or portals. Lift the shell up a few inches and tilt it toward you slightly, so that the far rigger doesn't scratch the boat below it as you back up and walk the shell away from the rack. From here you can either roll it down to your waist or employ one of the following overhead carries.

The Arm Carry

Once you have walked the boat away from the rack, you should press it over your head and lock your elbows to support it. If your boat is built without a comfortable place between the tracks to rest it on your head you may want to walk it to the water as is, keeping both of your arms fully extended. This method requires a fair amount of arm strength and/or a light boat, but it is a no-nonsense carry that allows you to roll the shell right in when you reach the water. If you use this method, make sure the handles or portals fore and aft of the seat tracks are quite sturdy, in case a good breeze comes along.

The Head Carry

This classic carry uses your head to support the weight of the boat. Some people shy away from this technique, because it can be genuinely uncomfortable the first few tries. However, it is an effective method once you get a sense of where on your head the boat should go, and how to place the boat there so that it balances. When you find these two balance points—the one on your head and the other on the boat—it generally won't feel all that heavy or uncomfortable.

The trick lies in knowing where on your head the boat should go and how to place the boat there so it balances. Balancing the boat is key, because if the boat starts to lean one way or the other, it will suddenly feel twice as heavy. From the arm-carry position, you simply lower the shell down to the top of your head. When you do find the right balance point, your arms are now free to grab the riggers and keep the boat level bow to stern and port to starboard, without having to support the boat's weight (see fig. 1). This setup is especially good in windy conditions, because the arms can help tilt the hull toward the wind.

If possible, you should have someone spot you the first several times you attempt this carry. That way, if something goes wrong, you won't drop the shell or wrench your neck.

The Shoulder Carry

Popularized in Europe, this right-side-up carry is a good one for bigger rowers. Hoist the boat up onto one shoulder by palming the bottom of the hull with one hand and holding the gunwale with the other. The hull is then cradled in the space between your neck and shoulder, cushioned by the trapezius muscle. If you don't have any cushion in your neck or the one-armed strength to hoist the boat, this carry isn't for you. Also keep in mind that many boats made with delicate hull materials don't take kindly to a bony shoulder.

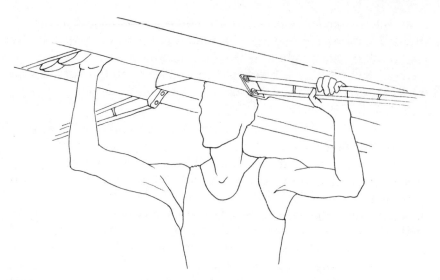

Fig. 1

For tall rowers, this method has the added practical benefit of keeping the boat below head level, where it won't crash into a low entryway or boat-bay door.

Carrying Bigger Boats

Some boats are quite heavy and can't be carried alone. If you row out of a busy boat club, you generally won't have a problem finding someone to help you out. When you carry a boat with two people, especially a double scull, remember that it is generally a bad idea to hold it at the very ends, unless the manufacturer has put the handles there. This places a great deal of stress on the middle of the boat. You will better preserve the boat's stiffness if you support it halfway between the ends and the cockpit, much the same way a good rack supports it.

Other options exist. Many people who own wider recreational boats on lakes or ponds just drag them ashore and tie them up. This is okay if the hull is sturdy enough and doesn't have a fin that can break off. Other people buy strap-on wheel systems that allow them to haul the heavy boats up to a garage or shed. A third option is to buy or make a boat with a removable rigging unit, like the popular Alden Ocean Shell. This divides the weight in half; of course, you have to put the rig together every time you use it. Still, if you aren't that strong, or if you have to load your boat on top of your car regularly, removable rigging may be something to consider.

GETTING IN AND OUT OF A SHELL

Serious damage can be done to a delicate boat—synthetic or wooden—if it is entered incorrectly. The classic mistake of stepping directly into the bottom of a shell generally results in either a foot-sized hole or a nasty crack.

Dreading the destruction of their handiwork, older boat-builders sometimes addressed this problem by putting the message "Do not step here" in the bottom of the shell. Nowadays, synthetic boats often feature added reinforcement in places where careless rowers may tread. At any rate, learning the right way to enter and exit a shell will hold you in good stead regardless of the vintage or make of the boat. Described below is the classic way to step into a single, although other options exist.

If your leg strength is good and your knees are serviceable, the maneuver is something like a one-legged knee bend (see fig. 2). Holding on to both oar handles with the hand nearest the water, push the sliding seat toward the bow with your other hand or your foot and step into the sternmost center section of the seat platform, right in between the seat tracks. Many boats actually have a step plate or at least a textured skid pad indicating where the foot should go.

Before you lower yourself down onto the seat, make sure that it has returned to a position just behind your heel. As you bend at the knee, also bend at the waist to maintain your balance. Your free foot can swing directly to the footboard, where it rests lightly. Your free hand can help support your weight by resting on the dock. The gunwales of most fine racing singles should not be used to help support your descending body weight. Some people, however, like to grab the rigger arm or even the oarlock pin, which is also fine.

This simple maneuver can prove difficult for many on the first few tries. If you want to look like a real rower, stick with it. Of course, you can use other, less elegant techniques. One method is to sit down beside your boat and basically shuffle your butt onto the seat, supporting your body weight briefly with your hand on the dock. I don't recommend this method because you risk landing on the gunwale in transit, but some folks with knee injuries, for exam-

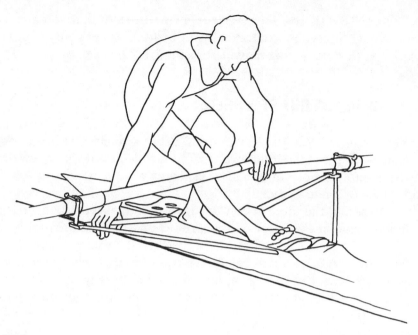

Fig. 2

ple, don't have much of a choice. As with all entries, remember to always keep your other hand on the oar handles to keep your boat stable.

Don't fret too much if you aren't particularly graceful getting in and out of your shell. It's what you do on the water that counts!

LAUNCHING AND LANDING

Even at the major rowing camps, this part of basic boatmanship is largely glossed over, leaving many novices stuck uncomfortably in the docking area, requiring a push off or a pull in and inviting the possibility of damage to the shells.

If you launch from a short dock, you may have gotten away with just sliding off the end when departing, and inching your way in the opposite direction on your return. Sooner or later, however, you may find yourself in the middle of a long, crowded dock, and this technique just won't do. Imagine not being able to launch and land from an awards dock to accept your medal!

Don't laugh. Even experienced scullers, faced with a dock where they can't just slide on and off the end, are often caught looking a little foolish. So here's what to do.

Launching

Most novices try to shove the boat sideways, straight away from the dock. This move only gets them a few feet clear and leaves them in a position where they must pull in their dockside oar and use it to push off or "pole away" from the dock, just like eights and fours do. The problem with this technique is that, in a single, shipping in one of your two oars is a dicey move that places all of your balance solely on the waterside oar. It's doable, but there is a more stable and graceful way.

Remember, boats are designed to go forward, not sideways, which is why a sideways shove doesn't get you where you want to go. Instead try pushing in a forward, diagonal direction as you lean away from the dock and slightly square your waterside oar. When you do this, hold both of your grips in your waterside hand, to free up your pushing hand and still have control of both oars. With a fairly easy push, a slight lean, and a little patience, the boat will pivot away and completely clear the dock. Even with a tentative shove that gets you halfway there, all you have to do is come up the slide to the catch, and your dockside oar will reach the water. Tap it away with a few short strokes.

Landing

Landing is done using the same glide-and-pivot principle as the shove described above. Paddle lightly toward the dock at about a 30 degree angle, taking into account the direction and force of the wind (you'll need a little more power coming in against the wind, and a little less coming in with it). When you are about a boat length away from the dock, stop rowing and push your oar handles down into your lap. Lean away from the dock so that your boat will gently begin to pivot on the waterside blade, while the other oar lifts up over the dock.

If you find yourself coming in at too sharp an angle or too fast, just square up a little on the waterside blade you are leaning onto and the boat will pivot sooner. You will need a little practice to get the speed and the timing of the lean just right, but you are better off erring on the conservative side, coming parallel too abruptly and doing a "fly-by," rather than ramming the dock. Despite what some coxswains and scullers may think, bows and bow balls were not designed as a boat's landing gear. Accordingly, you shouldn't rub or scrape them along the dock to bring yourself into position. Likewise, oars weren't meant to either fend off or brake your landings, so don't let them scrape along the dock. Instead, try to glide in without touching the dock with your boat or your oars, coming to a full stop before gently laying down the dockside oar.

Some books and camps like to teach a stern-first landing method, which has the benefit of allowing you to see your approach better. This is also a better method to use on short docks, which aren't much bigger than the length of your boat. You must have excellent **backing** skills (see below) and good balance to do this maneuver, but you should learn it at some point in your sculling career, since it gives you yet another option. You perform the stern-first landing the same way as the one described above, except that you are pointing your stern in at a 30 degree angle, rather than your bow. When you lean away from the dock, remember that you should only half-feather the waterside oar, instead of letting it return to its flat spot in the oarlock. Otherwise, traveling in reverse, the blade will dive and you will flip. I like to use the stern-first landing when it faces me back into the wind, since as every small boat owner knows, it is easier to land into a wind than with it.

BACKING

Being able to move your boat backward is a good skill to learn not only for landings but for general maneuvering purposes. If you watch the Olympics or the World Championships, you'll see the boats back up into their starting blocks or stake boats. If you plan to race in sprints, you'll need to learn to do this as well, although there are plenty of good scullers who show up at their first race unable to perform this skill. Even if you don't plan on racing, backing is a worthwhile thing to learn.

You can hold your blades two different ways when you back-stroke, depending on whether you own traditional (macon) blades—the symmetrical type—or the modern hatchet variety. In either case, the body motion is the same. Beginning at the finish, you are going to push your blades away from you by pulling yourself forward with your feet—a no-no in the forward direction. Your arms, back, and legs will move in the same normal order as if you were executing a stroke's return.

If you have traditional-shaped blades, you should turn them around into a reverse position; if you have hatchets, you will keep them positioned normally. At the end of the backing stroke, where your body is normally in its catch position, feather by rolling the oar handles away from you slightly so that they skim smoothly along the water's surface as you pull them back to your waist. If you have only a short distance to cover or wish to move quite slowly, leave your legs flat and use only your arms.

HOW TO LOOK BEHIND YOU

I've found that very few recreational scullers know how to turn around to look behind them without upsetting their balance or the rhythm of their stroke. While the timing of this technique takes practice, it allows you to integrate the head turn smoothly into your rowing. Begin turning your head just after you've planted your catch (but *not* before), and then let your shoulders twist a little, if necessary, through mid-drive, right through to the finish. Starting right after the catch like this allows you a pretty leisurely head and shoulder turn, as well as the ability to move your hands right around the finish and not have them stop dead in your lap. If you wait until the finish to try to whip your head around, you'll not only end up stopping the stroke there but will risk disrupting your balance and rushing your slide to get to the next stroke.

You may want to initially learn to look over only one shoulder. However, you will need to be able to look over both shoulders equally well. Naturally, how often you turn around depends on numerous variables, lessened somewhat by your familiarity with the course. I might add that knowing the body of water that you row on is no substitute for turning around to check your course. Too many scullers get lazy once they think they know their daily route. You have to remember that water is not a stable terrain; currents and breezes can quickly shift your position. Also, you never know when some piece of debris or strange animal may suddenly appear off your bow.

Mirrors

While there is no substitute for turning around to see where you are going, many veteran scullers swear by tiny rearview mirrors that dangle from a hat or a headband and allow you to keep facing sternward. The case for using a mirror is that you don't have to worry about disrupting your stroke by taking a glance behind you. If you have poor neck or back flexibility, turning around can indeed be a real chore, and if done awkwardly, it can affect both power and balance. Mirror users claim that with practice—often an entire season's worth—you'll never have to turn around again. These mirrors can be purchased at any bicycle shop and fastened to the frame of your sunglasses, close enough to your face so that you have a sufficiently large field of vision.

Compass and GPS

The other directional aid used, especially in open-water rowing, is a stern-mounted compass. In the ocean or on a large lake, where bearings are few and far between, you may need to keep your course with a compass. Of course, a compass can't account for currents and winds that may slide you sideways.

Any serious kayaker who takes to the ocean also carries along a map and a tide chart, which is a smart idea for anyone venturing far ashore. Open-water racers have taken to using electronic GPS (global positioning system) units, which work off satellites to tell you exactly where you are on the water.

STEERING

Steering and turning the boat around can be the cause of some consternation for novice scullers. If you are rowing in an intermediate or racing shell, you may want to go back and practice these techniques in a wider boat, so that you can work on the maneuver without fear of capsizing.

Oar Pressure

The obvious way to alter your course is to simply pull harder on one oar. When you apply pressure to the starboard or port oar, remember two important things. First, power should still be initiated from the legs; second, your blades are going to turn the boat more at the beginning of the stroke than at the end. These two concerns are related, but let's take them separately.

Pushing Off the Footboard

A common novice mistake in trying to change course is to use the arms too early, breaking the elbows, literally trying to pull the boat around. Some beginners actually have to stop rowing and use their arms exclusively to get repositioned. However, you do not need to alter the basic mechanics of your stroke just to alter your course.

Remember, your legs are stronger than your arms and should always be set in motion first. Also, in order to use the legs most effectively, you have to keep your arms and your grip relatively relaxed. If you grab with your arms, or even hold too tightly to the oar you wish to power with, you essentially interrupt your leg drive and prevent it from contributing properly to the stroke. With this in mind, don't think of *pulling* harder with one oar but of *pushing* harder with the leg on the same side.

Applying Pressure at the Catch

While you focus on your feet as you bring the boat around, also think about applying your power to the oar as soon as it touches the water. At the catch, the blade has much more mechanical ability to push the bow over and change its direction. Much less is gained by trying to accelerate the oar toward the end of the stroke, and you may get caught up in the upper-body "hauling" syndrome described above. Its also rather exhausting on the arms, and in a long head race you don't want them to get cramped up. Again, taking full advantage of the legs, some scullers even cut their finishes short and negotiate a tight turn with a series of quick, powerful bursts at the catch.

Altering the Catch Angles

When you are faced with a big bend in the river, you may find that applying pressure to one oar is not enough to bring the boat around. To get more turning power, you can shorten up the reach of the oar

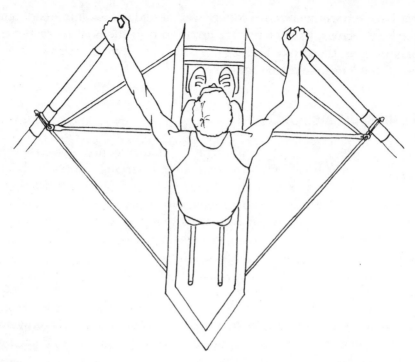

Fig. 3

nearest the inside of the turn (see fig. 3). After you put this oar in the water, virtually let it drift. That way your other oar, taking its normal course and speed through the water, has enough time to catch up by the time it reaches the finish. Thus, even though the two oars are entering the water at different angles, they will still come out together.

It may feel weird at first to put your blades in the water at asymmetrical angles, but this technique is a very effective way of bringing a boat around a sharp turn. The technique works on the previously mentioned principle of applying pressure to the blades while they are at the tightest angle to the bow. The inner oar, placed in the water short and weak, is doing little other than keeping the boat from flipping.

TURNING THE BOAT AROUND

The basic turning method of rowing with one oar while resting the other one flat on the water is the easiest to master. Pull the unused oar handle in to your waist and hold it there, so it will not get in the way while you row with the other oar. Initially, it may also help to press it down toward your thigh, and lean toward it a little bit. Row with only your back and arms; keep your legs flat.

This technique works well when you want to work your way across the river as you turn the boat. It isn't very good for tight spots that don't afford such a wide turning radius. When you can accomplish this technique comfortably, try making a tighter turn by squaring the unused oar and letting it drag in the water. With the blade squared, you don't want to lean excessively onto the buried oar, as it will no longer support you as well as it did when feathered.

For turning in place, you'll need to learn how to alternate a back stroke with a forward stroke. Begin at the finish, with both oar handles at your waist, and both blades feathered flat on the water. Square one blade into a backing position. Now slowly push both hands away from you, backing with the one oar and keeping the other feathered. As you approach the catch position, feather the oar you just backstroked with and take a regular, forward stroke with the other one. When you feather the backing oar, make sure you let it roll only halfway, so that it will surf on top of the water as you re-trieve it (just as in backing). You can turn in place this way using your legs, or just using your back and arms.

GETTING BACK INTO A CAPSIZED BOAT

At the Craftsbury Sculling Center, before you can even go rowing for the first time the instructors make you capsize and re-enter your boat. The flip test is done right off the dock in front of all the other campers, and it can be a rather sobering experience for a first outing. However, the ability to re-enter a capsized boat is a valuable one to learn.

Righting the Shell

Oddly enough, when you flip a shell, it usually remains upright. All you need do is bring the oar handles together and execute the re-entry procedure described below. If the shell has turned over, how-ever, you can right it by reaching over the top of the hull and grabbing the rigger or gunwale on the opposite side. Place your other hand on the rigger right beside you and push down as you pull

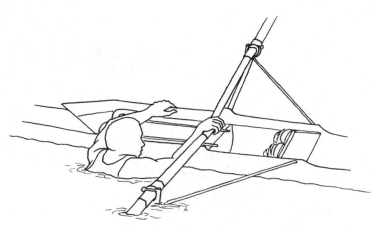

Fig. 4

the far rigger toward you. If you are trying to right a wide, recreational shell, or your arms just aren't long enough, you may have to actually stand on the near rigger to initiate this maneuver.

Re-Entry

When the boat is upright and you are positioned along its starboard side, bring the oar-handle grips together into your right hand and press them down against the seat deck or the footstretcher. If the far oar has swung out of reach, you'll have to pull yourself up onto the boat a bit to reach it (see fig. 4). Grab the far gunwale with your left hand and pull your torso up into the cockpit so that it is suspended across the two gunwales (fig. 5). Now, using a dolphin or scissors kick for momentum give a quick pivot or twist with your hips as you pull yourself the remainder of the way, so that you end up sitting on the seat deck. Quickly raise the oar handles, lowering the blades to the water, to regain balance (fig. 6). Now shuffle your legs into the boat, holding on to the gunwale with your left hand. Find the seat and get back on it by supporting yourself with your left hand on the seat deck behind you.

Swimming the Boat to Shore

Although learning how to get back into a capsized shell is a valuable skill, you should not subject yourself or your boat to any unnecessary

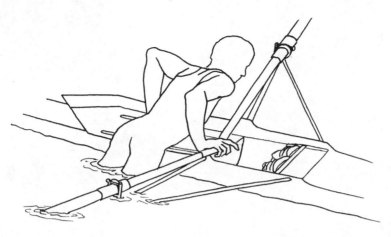

Fig. 5

abuse. The method described above is not easy, and I've seen even strong rowers end up with bruised upper bodies (not to mention egos) while trying to accomplish it. Also, keep in mind that many rowing shells are delicately built. If you throw your body up onto the gunwales of some boats, you will definitely risk damaging them. Given these factors, it is sometimes wiser to swim the boat to shallow water, using a gentle sidestroke, and re-enter it there the normal way.

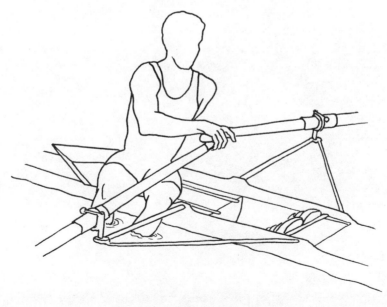

Fig. 6

Boat-Handling Skills

One veteran sculler you don't want to mess with—Ted Anderson.

CHAPTER 5

DEVELOPING TECHNIQUE AND POWER

The best thing for rowing is rowing.

—Calvin Coffey

Y ou've learned how to scull, or at least progressed to the point where you can keep your oars off the water during the recovery and put some pressure on them during the drive. Perhaps you rowed sweeps in college and this process has only taken a few months, or even a few weeks. Now you find yourself wondering what the challenge of sculling is all about. Perhaps you should enter some races, you think, and put your skills to the test. Then one day you're out on the river, paddling along, and an old duffer shoves off just ahead of you in a wooden boat. His tousled white hair and old gray sweatshirt make him look like a physics professor on the loose from the local university. Nevertheless, instead of waiting for you to go by, he starts paddling along right in front of you.

You chuckle inwardly. This old guy thinks he can actually match strokes with you. Okay, you say to yourself, I'll play along for a while. Instead of powering right by him, you decide to pick up the pressure gradually, pressing the ancient mariner until he can't take it any longer. Your plan is a little cruel perhaps, but he asked for it, cutting right in front of you like that. You begin with a firm paddle, keeping a relaxed grip on the oars, and getting into a rhythm. After a minute or so you take a look ahead and see that he is still there, about twenty strokes ahead of you. You pick it up to half pressure for a few minutes, and for a moment you think you notice the puddles of his oars drawing nearer. You don't need to turn around; you can feel that he is right in front of you now, but you're going to press your bow right up to his stern and act as if you didn't even know he was there. Devious but delightful at the same time.

Suddenly, you don't feel his puddles cuffing your hull anymore, and you look ahead to see that somehow the professor is now some forty strokes ahead of you. So he's got a little kick in him after all. Abandoning your initial plan, you pick up your stroke rating and put full pressure on the oars. Enough of this game—it's time to dispense with this guy. He's beginning to get on your nerves. Another two minutes go by and you still haven't caught him. Your forearms are starting to cramp up and you realize that you've been gripping the oars too tightly. As you try to relax, you realize that you've abandoned technique in favor of raw power, and it isn't working. You're barely making progress on old man river.

Somehow he's still out there, just in front of you, chugging along at a steady clip. Your boat is now lurching and checking as you power it along. Your finishes are rough; the blades are either washing out or crabbing. You have closed the gap between you and your opponent, but you are at the very limits of your aerobic fitness. Lactic acid has already started to seep into your legs and shellac your quadriceps with pain. Worse than this, you suddenly realize that quite possibly you played right into the old man's plan, and not vice versa. With every stroke, you get more and more frustrated as this thought takes hold. Finally you stop, short of breath and out of patience. You can't bear to look ahead and see him still rowing, acknowledging how hard you have been pulling to no avail.

As you turn around to head back home, suddenly you hear a voice: "Not bad, but you need to learn to take the turns a little better." The professor comes paddling up beside you and now you notice that his arms and legs are sinewy and quite strong. Beneath his leathery skin lies a set of lean muscles that look like wound steel cable. You paddle along together for a while in silence, and you notice how he takes fewer, more relaxed strokes to keep pace with you. He doesn't appear to use much power as he pulls the oars through the water, and there is no rushed or jerky movement of his body between strokes. His boat moves very steadily through the water, as if an invisible rope is pulling it along. Yours seems to surge and stall. He is almost mechanical in his sense of rhythm, which seems to come from a strong internal focus. You need to look out of your boat a lot more, and you let steering, wind, and water conditions interfere with your concentration. In short, he does less and gets more.

So how did he get to be so good? Time on the water, people have told you. But what does this mean exactly? What should be happening during this mysterious incubation process, so that you too develop into a master sculler? It helps, especially if you don't have a coach, to have some general sense of what you should be thinking about during this developmental stage. Some of these more subtle themes provide the discussion for the first part of this chapter: blending power and technique, learning to relax, developing a sense of internal focus. The second half talks about taking these skills with you when you start rowing with other scullers. Whether you are looking to eventually compete against others or just yourself, you will do well to reflect on the internal skills before you get too involved with the more external distractions of the sport.

A PORTRAIT OF THE SCULLER AS AN ATHLETE

The above episode with the veteran sculler isn't just a hypothetical fable. It happened to me early in my sculling career, and in one form or another, it has happened to countless other scullers. Hopefully it will happen to you. Why? If you are ever going to compete, or row your best, you need to be beaten by someone you perceive to be weaker than you to realize what power is all about. And the comparison doesn't have to be young versus old for the same lesson to be learned. It can be male versus female, or lightweight versus heavyweight. I once coached a young British sculler who stood about six foot six and weighed nearly two hundred pounds. A graduate student and former sweep rower into his second year of sculling, he was starting to move a single well enough to handle most of the scullers on the Charles. Young and cocky, he decided to go to the Henley Royal Regatta in England to try his luck in the prestigious Diamond Sculls event. Unfortunately for him, he drew the eventual winner, Willem Von Bellingham, in his first race.

Von Bellingham probably weighed no more than 170 pounds and stood no higher than my young friend's shoulder. We noticed this after the race, when the Belgian had won by that margin the

TRANSITIONING FROM SWEEP ROWING TO SCULLING

If you rowed crew in college you already know the basic body motion of the rowing stroke, as well as a general feel for balancing a boat and applying the oars to the water. There are, however, some subtle differences between sculling and sweep rowing that must be learned if you aspire to reach the higher competitive levels of the sport. A majority of scullers on the U.S. National Team are former sweep rowers who took up sculling after their college careers. Despite their excellent fitness, many of them don't succeed against their European rivals, who often begin sculling in their adolescent years.

Single sculling, which demands a unique set of boat skills and a strong individualistic character, is almost diametrically opposed to team rowing, where everyone must follow one another. Generally, a mature single sculler possesses the combined team attributes of a stroke, a coxswain, and a coach, and must have an excellent sense of pacing and steering, as well as at least a working knowledge of training and rigging.

British simply call "easily." The seasoned lightweight handled my friend as a cat handles a mouse. After the race, he approached us and, in broken English with a big smile on his face, explained: "You see, you do not need to be big to go fast. I am small. You are big. I win." Keeping a winsome smile on his own face for the Belgian champ, my young charge subsequently hightailed it over to the food tent to drown his sorrows in Pimm's and clotted cream. His day would come, but not that afternoon.

Rethinking Power

Power for many rowers is defined as sheer force. If you look in the dictionary, however, the first definition of *power* is actually "the ability or capacity to perform or act effectively." Only the third definition mentions anything about strength or force, but somehow most of us end up dwelling on that one. Our egos love big displays of personal force—the gut-wrenching, muscle-bulging, "Look at me, I'm rowing hard" type of power.

Your boat couldn't care less about such raw displays of power. In fact, it doesn't particularly like disruptive movement, the kind that usually comes with this gut-wrenching effort. What it wants is to travel along at a steady clip, as if there was a light breeze behind it, blowing it along at a constant speed. In order to allow your scull this kind of motion, you have to develop the sensitivity of your own movements back and forth along the slide. To a raw-power type of person, this can be counterintuitive.

BLENDING POWER AND TECHNIQUE

The time-for-distance workout below is an example of a way to develop your technique and power at the same time. Curiously

ROWING TIME FOR DISTANCE

One way to gain a better sense of smooth, efficient movement is to see how much distance you can cover given a set amount of time. The interval can last anywhere from 30 to 90 minutes, and ideally you'll use about 75 percent of your maximum power. Most people try to use 100 percent of their maximum power when they want to cover more distance over a period of time. There is nothing wrong with this once you have truly developed your technique. If you haven't, however, you'll probably end up rowing these pieces as if you were on a rowing machine, with less regard for the way the boat is moving than for how hard you can push yourself to the edge.

Again, there's nothing wrong with going flat out. But rowing time for distance at slightly less than maximum pressure will allow you to focus on and develop the elements of an efficient stroke while still getting in a decent workout. Your mind will be focused on getting the most out of each stroke, allowing the boat to cover as much water between each catch as possible, rather than simply pulling hard against the clock. With this workout, which can be done a few times a week, you will not only learn how to make your movements efficient but also start to feel how smoothly the boat moves through the water.

enough, people with little or no athletic aspirations often develop technical proficiency in a scull more quickly. Unhampered by the need to showcase their physical prowess, these people approach sculling as they might approach learning to play a musical instrument—less with their muscles than with their mind. For these people, sculling is more of an aesthetic endeavor than an athletic one. They have seen the beauty of the sculling motion and want to be a part of it in the same way that a musician becomes a part of the music. They look forward to the technical challenges of the sport as the necessary steps toward this synthesis, not as frustrations that get in the way of their desire to work up a sweat or encounter pain.

In the end, power and technique are really just two sides of the same coin and need to be practiced in tandem. The reason is partly psychological. If you associate technique only with light strokes, it may not be there when you start taking hard strokes. Some people do the opposite. They row poorly on the paddle and then focus on technique only during their fast pieces. Ideally, you should try to row well on all your strokes, and not alter or summon your technique only at certain times. In a sense, technique should be like a special set of clothes that you put on when you go sculling. Always dress yourself in a state of technical awareness. At first, these new clothes may feel cumbersome or restrictive. After a while, you'll forget about the clothes, but they will still be there.

Learning How to Relax

When you first learn any new movement, you're bound to be a little tense. In sculling, tension is certainly required to generate motion, but only at the right time, in the right muscles.

As I mentioned in the chapter on equipment, you can spare yourself a lot of unnecessary tension by choosing a boat that isn't too difficult for you to handle. You should always feel free to move back into a more stable boat to work on relaxation and power. There you will be able to pull hard unimpeded by the extra tension and effort brought on by instability. Rowing in a heavier boat like a wherry can also be an excellent way to build rowing muscles during the early season, in lieu of weights.

Especially if you are a power rower—someone who likes to pull hard—going out and doing just that in a stable boat for a

PYRAMID TRAINING: SMALL PACKAGES OF POWER AND TECHNIQUE

Another good workout for developing power and technique in tandem is known as a pyramid workout. This training method is especially good for those who may have not been former athletes in other sports and want to develop more boat speed or a higher level of cardiovascular fitness. The total duration of the workout can be anywhere from 30 to 60 minutes, depending on how fit you are to begin with, but unlike the previous exercise it is not a "steady state" type of workout. Instead, it is a series of short bursts of power: ten strokes hard, followed by ten strokes easy; then twenty strokes hard, followed by twenty strokes easy; then thirty strokes hard, followed by thirty strokes easy. Then the whole cycle begins again.

As you do the easy strokes, even though you may be tired, think of being technically precise instead of letting everything fall apart. As you build into the hard strokes, take this composure with you and try to remain relaxed but poised. Push yourself on the hard strokes, but not beyond the point where exhaustion and tension will take control and compromise your technique. As you get more fit, you'll be able to push harder without losing your composure.

Another way to do pyramids, which is less mechanical but demands a little more internal awareness and discipline, is called a natural pyramid. Paddle along at solid half pressure, focusing on taking long, smooth strokes. Then gradually begin to take the pressure up toward full, until you reach the point where exhaustion and tension are about to take over and compromise the integrity of your stroke. Become aware of this physical boiling point. It is known as your *anaerobic threshold,* the point at which you will have exhausted the oxygen-utilizing (aerobic) process in your muscles and begin to rely on other, more painful, and less efficient anaerobic processes. Slowly back down off that point, easing the pressure back to a comfortable half pressure. When you feel rested, take the pressure up gradually again.

season or two is one way to become efficient and strong. For this reason a lot of sculling clubs require their novice scullers to accumulate a certain amount of miles in a wherry or gig. A great British sculler named Jack Beresford pointed out that this type of long, slow mileage is required to hone technique, for "one only learns how to scull when tired." Initially, until you become adept, it generally takes a few miles of hard rowing before you begin to relax and use only those muscles and movements essential to moving the boat.

It takes time to develop a sense of discrimination on all of these fronts, to know when and where it is necessary to tense or relax, when to hold your body firm or when to release it. The longer you row, the better able you will be to identify places of unnecessary tension and then eliminate it from your stroke.

THE PICK DRILL

Another way to relax is to mentally identify the different muscles used to propel the boat and relax them one by one as you begin your warm-up. I often us the "pick drill" to do this, even though it is more commonly used to teach beginners how to row. Basically it breaks the stroke down into the use of arms, then arms and back, then arms, back, and legs. Beginning with just arms, I make sure my hands are relaxed. Adding the back, I'll make sure the shoulders aren't tense. Adding the legs, I'll feel the resistance travel up from the lower back, through the lats, the shoulders, the biceps, the forearms, and the hands without any blockage from tension held too long in any one part.

Identifying your rowing muscles is also a good way to feel all the linkages that run through the legs, the back, and the arms. I focus on the upper body because it is a natural place for me to hold tension. If you tune in to your body, you may identify other areas of unnecessary tension—including the feet, which occasionally try to aid balance by tensing individually.

INTERNAL FOCUS: KEEPING YOUR MIND IN YOUR BOAT

Willpower, inner strength, visualization ability—these are terms used to describe the traits of someone who has internal focus. Beginning rowers have very little ability to focus within themselves, because they are so preoccupied with the various external matters of technique. Until the basics are mastered, it is nearly impossible to keep a steady internal focus, which shows in the overall integrity of your stroke. Once you have gained enough mastery of technique so that you can relax, however, you should begin developing a sense of internal awareness and focus.

Close Your Eyes

Try closing your eyes in a stable boat or on a rowing machine and see how many strokes you can take before you feel tippy or out of rhythm. This drill will provide you with a kernel of the inner concentration I'm talking about. The goal here is for the mind and the oars to be in synch and free from the constant worry of visual distractions. The expression "keep your mind in your own boat" refers to the type of concentration required to allow you and your boat to become one efficient orchestration of movements in the face of external distractions, particularly during competition.

Watch Others, Watch Yourself

Another thing you can do is simply to watch others who have this blend of concentration and grace. I'm not suggesting that you copy their technique down to the minutest detail, just that you observe and absorb the general elements of their power and grace. If you don't have anyone impressive around, try watching videos of some great contemporary scullers to absorb some of the rhythm and integrity of their movements. One of the best male models ever put on film was the Russian Vyasheslav Ivanov; one of the best female scullers was the German Christine Schelbilch.

If you have the opportunity, you should also get yourself on video. Keeping a video and/or written record of your own rowing from season to season can be very helpful. With a video in hand, you or your coach can bring into alignment the external picture of your rowing and the internal picture you imagine as you row. Sometimes you may fall back into bad habits that are more easily corrected by having a look at your journal and/or video. More often it is just fun and inspiring to watch how much stronger and more graceful you become as time goes by.

With internal awareness comes better boat awareness, or an almost intuitive sense of how the boat is moving through the water. The numerous physical and mental tasks required to scull well may at first seem like an impossible juggling act that will never come together. Eventually, however, you will begin to feel it as a total synchronicity of mind, muscle, and boat, with less and less distinction between the three. With the passing of time, your fitness in a boat will naturally improve, as your body becomes more and more accustomed to the specific demands of the rowing stroke. Likewise, you will become more adept at handling the boat and the oars.

EXTERNAL FOCUS: MOVING OUTSIDE YOURSELF

Remember your friend the old sculler? Are you ready to show him the new power and efficiency in your stroke? Perhaps you have a rematch in mind, where you can finally put him in his place. Not so fast. Even though you've worked hard on your stroke, you haven't practiced these new skills side by side with another sculler. The professor was not only more efficient and more focused than you, he was also a clever competitor who stayed right in front of you, where he could gauge your every move and respond without you noticing. When you put the power on, so did he. When you relaxed, he eased off as well. He was rowing in a superior position, playing off your power. It would have been almost impossible for you to pass without exerting an enormous effort.

Some of the following strategies are basic racing skills, but they will serve anyone who wants to improve their rowing.

Find a Paddling Partner

If you have been training on your own for a while and feel like your technique and fitness have reached a plateau, you may want to search out the company of other scullers. Try to find a person or a small group who has the same general goals as you do and who works out at roughly around your speed or slightly faster. It makes little sense to try to row with the real sharks on the river when you are still a guppie.

If you are lucky, you'll find a paddling partner who you can row with for miles without straying too far apart. In a very relaxed fashion, you can get the practice of being quite near another sculler without losing the integrity of your stroke. Rowing with another person demands another level of concentration that is difficult if you haven't gained enough intuitive sense of your stroke. Part of your mind needs to be attending to your partner, but enough of it still needs to be in your own boat. At first you may feel awkward, but when you get the hang of it, you'll find rowing with a partner can be invigorating and a wonderful way to go out and click off the miles.

Some scullers like to chat on these partner rows, while others develop them into more serious training sessions. When you are comfortable with each other and aren't clashing your oars together every ten strokes, you can practice trading the lead for different stretches of water. One way to do this is to have the trailing sculler gradually pick up the power for a short period or until her stern reaches your bow. This leapfrogging approach is a kind of two-person pyramid-style workout. Once you've gotten used to rowing together like this, you can do any number of interesting workouts, with set intervals of different lengths and durations.

Sometimes rowing with just one person all the time can become redundant. It can also be frustrating if one of you is always faster than the other and both of you are working your way toward a competitive goal. For this reason, I encourage partner rowing as a long, slow, noncompetitive distance workout a few times a week, where both people stay together through the duration of the practice.

Train in a Double

Another way to enhance your training and technical proficiency in a single is to find a good double-scull partner. Again, choosing the right person is important; you don't want someone who is either way behind or way ahead of you in terms of ability. On the other hand, you needn't choose someone who is completely compatible with you in temperament, technique, or single-scull speed. Some degree of contrast in both personality and rowing style can make for a fruitful exchange. Some of the best competitive doubles have in fact been composed of rather unlikely duos.

A coach can help you identify a doubles partner and work with you to mesh your styles. Typically, one sculler will be stronger technically, and the other may generate more raw power. If both athletes can borrow from each other's strengths, they can figure out more quickly what makes a boat go fast. In most doubles, the more technically inclined sculler should sit in the bow seat and take on the added role of steersman, while the more powerful sculler should be placed in the stroke's seat. Initially, however, you should switch seats a few times and just get comfortable with each other.

You also need to get comfortable with the double itself, which will travel much more quickly than a single. As a result, your catch and finish reflexes will sharpen and become quicker, and the way you apply power will generally smooth out. Needless to say, this experience will ultimately benefit the way both of you row in singles. Again, choose your partner wisely (e.g., don't just pick a friend or spouse) and try to have a coach on hand for those times when things get frustrating.

Teach Beginners

Even if you haven't perfected your sculling (if that is ever possible), coaching beginners can be a valuable experience that will accelerate your own progress. Like watching videos, coaching forces you to carefully observe the mechanics of the human body as it tries to accomplish this rather odd motion we know as sculling. When you have to verbalize your observations to a total novice, you will receive yet another perspective on the sport, a way of developing a critical distance from something you may be passionately engrossed in. This perspective is something you will need to apply to your own sculling if you want to improve more rapidly. With every sculler you teach, you'll gain a deeper understanding of the subtle physical challenges of sculling and hopefully be able to apply them to your own stroke.

Be Patient

Whether you are looking to compete against others or just yourself, you will undoubtedly reach points in your sculling career where your enthusiasm and ambition overrun your ability. Those moments can be frustrating indeed, but don't beat yourself up too much. Try to balance your passion with patience. Keep your motivation going and let it develop into a gradual, long-range plan. Get together with a coach or an experienced sculler, and figure out some general goals at the beginning of the season. And don't let occasional defeat get you down. There will always be someone faster than you, as well as someone slower.

Andrew Black, an Australian sculler, in pursuit of the perfect catch.

CHAPTER 6

STRUCTURE AND FLOW

After due allowance is made for idiosyncrasies there can hardly be a doubt that, in such an art as that of oarsmanship there must be, for any given type of boat, some one method of propulsion which is best, both for obtaining speed and for sparing the oarsmen from unnecessary labour and exhaustion.

—*Gilbert C. Bourne*, A Textbook of Oarsmanship

Once you have put in enough time on the water to feel comfortable in a single, you may want to re-evaluate your technique with a little more scrutiny. "Ugh," you may groan, "but I thought I was done with technique!" As you progress with your sculling, you'll realize that the pursuit of technical excellence is never-ending. You may not be making big mistakes anymore, but there are places in your stroke that can be smoothed out. In the last chapter, you learned how to relax and allow things to come together. Now it's time to get a little analytical again. Chances are, if you've begun to watch other scullers and compare them to the way you look on video, this re-evaluation process has already begun.

In order to take a critical look at your own rowing or someone else's, you need to know a little bit more about the mechanics of the stroke and some of the common errors that other people make (not you, of course). The goal here is to maximize the physics of the human body. Good postural alignment provides both strength and fluidity, and while it may seem absurd to think that a small alteration in the way you hold or move your body can make a significant difference in your output, it most certainly can.

The first part of this chapter discusses some basic postural issues, and the second half lists some of the typical mistakes rowers often make due to misinterpretation of body mechanics. As you start scrutinizing, you'll be amazed at the different ways people move boats. Although it's important to have an understanding of the mechanics in order to improve, don't get too critical or hung up on achieving perfect form—it will inhibit your ability to maintain a sense of relaxation and fluidity.

MAKING BETTER CATCH AND FINISH TRANSITIONS

If you play a musical instrument, you may remember the difficult process of trying to connect chords or notes together so that the music flowed without hesitation. In rowing, you have only two chords to play: the drive and the recovery. The catch and the finish are the *transitions* between these two. Contrary to what some photographs make them look like, they are not rest stops where the music ceases to play; they are merely shifts in direction. The smoother you can make these shifts, the more evenly the movement of the boat will proceed. This is the true music of rowing. Some scullers even claim that they can hear or feel this movement by the way the water sounds against the hull.

From a postural perspective, you initially learn how to sit at the catch and the finish, and even pause at these two points to get ready for your blades' entry and exit from the water. It's time to stop sitting. Now you want to see how smoothly and quickly you can move around these areas of the stroke—not only by eliminating any hesitation in your bladework but by using your upperbody posture to anticipate moving in the opposite direction *before* the change in direction actually occurs. As you are completing the drive, for example, your head and shoulders should not be thrown back toward the bow (see fig. 1) but should remain level and bent over the oar handles (see fig. 2). This allows you to counterbalance your layback and achieve a more static position at the finish.

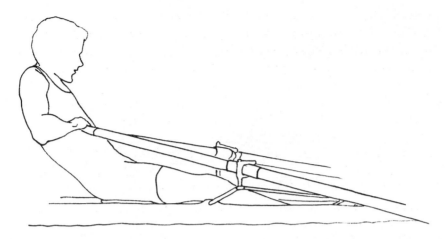

Fig. 1 Incorrect position

Coming forward, into the catch, the chin should rise so that the head remains level, and the back should straighten (see fig. 3) instead of feeling slouched over (see fig. 4). The shoulders should feel open and relaxed, ready to move in the opposite direction as soon as the oars touch the water. Again, the upper body should feel poised but relaxed just before the catch, not hunched, tight, or straining forward. In both the catch and the finish postures, the head and shoulders play

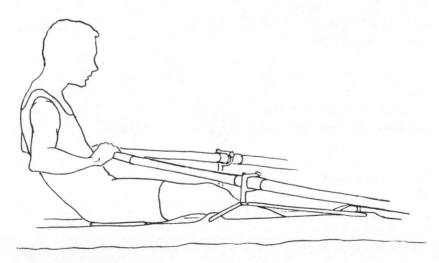

Fig. 2 Correct position

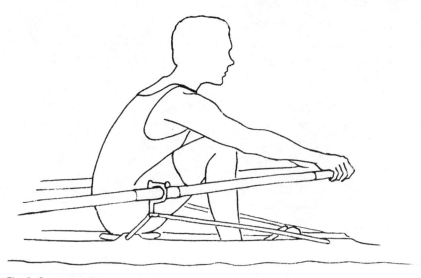

Fig. 3 Correct position

Fig. 4 Incorrect position

ROWING WITH YOUR FEET OUT OF THE SHOES

One drill to help you achieve smooth catch and finish transitions is to unfasten your feet and rest them on top of the shoes or clogs. With your feet unattached like this, you will need to negotiate your body weight into and out of the bow smoothly. This drill is especially good for those who tend to throw their weight into the bow in an unrestrained fashion. Doing this with the feet removed from the shoes will mean falling right out of the boat!

To prevent a dunking, you must not only restrict the quality and the amount of layback but learn to use the shoulders as a counterbalance. Coming into the final part of the drive, the shoulders must anticipate the change in direction the body will soon make, pulling themselves back over the oar handles. In this way, the body will achieve a more static posture at the finish, with less pressure on the stomach muscles and less need to pull with the feet to start moving the body out of the bow.

When you first try the drill, it may feel very odd and uncomfortable. After you learn to row "feet out," however, you'll find that your normal rowing will become noticeably smoother. I suggest using the drill as a daily warm-up, either by itself or in conjunction with other drills, such as the *half-slide pause drill* mentioned later in this chapter.

a vital role in leading the rest of the body out of the potential stopping point in the stroke. Because this poise is so important, I often tell scullers to row as if they had a book balanced on their head.

STRUCTURAL SYNDROMES

I mentioned earlier how a lack of good initial sculling instruction can often lead to bad habits. Like any other bad habit, the more you do it, the harder it is to change. If you're lucky, the solution may

THE CATCH DRILL

To practice the catch begin from a dead stop in a boat you can balance well. Sit at the finish position, with your blades buried and squared in the water. Making sure that the boat is perfectly balanced and that you are relaxed, initiate a stroke. Come up the slide as slowly as you can without letting your blades touch the water and stop moving just as the blades enter the water. You should be sitting in the catch postion, poised but relaxed, ready to take a stroke. In practicing this drill, some rowers like to consider the catch as the last part of the recovery, rather than the first part of the drive.

In addition to balance and body position, what you should focus on here is the quality of the catch, the feel and sound of it. If you have a coach, have your coach tell you how it looks. Most beginners try to place the blade in the water, which makes very little splash or sound, or jam it into the water by jerking the forearms up. In both cases, the grip on the oar will be tight. Relax the grip and let the blade fall into the water by virtue of gravity. It should make a gentle "pock" sound.

Remember that it helps to square up early so that you can relax your grip and forearms. Naturally the boat will be quite tippy sitting still in the water, so make sure you try this in a stable boat if you want to stay dry.

come by simply adjusting a basic postural issue like the two mentioned above; but sometimes the answer lies in addressing a combination of two or three interrelated areas of concern. Remember, the stroke is a fluid cycle composed of many connected parts; moving or changing one of these parts generally changes the entire construct of the stroke. To solve an ingrained problem in technique, you often have to address a few things simultaneously. In addition to posture, the sculler and/or coach must often re-examine how power is being applied, the relaxation and tension of muscles, and the correct coordination of the legs, back, and arms.

COMMON STRUCTURAL PROBLEMS IN THE DRIVE CYCLE

Most of these problems are "loose linkage" difficulties, which refers to the connections between the legs and the back and between the back and the arms. (Again, the mechanical metaphor is employed here.) While these syndromes are fairly easy to identify, solving them often requires a more comprehensive look at the entire stroke.

Throwing the Shoulders (Early Drive)

Perhaps the most common error among novice rowers is to lift or throw the shoulders toward the bow right at the beginning of the stroke. In an effort to set the stroke in motion, they swing their backs in a rowboat like manner before their legs have had a chance to do any work. This is also how most uninformed people row on the rowing machines installed at health clubs. Not only is throwing the shoulders potentially bad for the back, but it is also counterproductive in terms of smooth boat movement in a shell.

Remember, because of the sliding seat, the upper body merely plays a supporting role in the application of power. The legs are the real star of the show. They initiate the drive, and the back and arms follow through (see "Body Motion," in chapter 3). The back needs to support the drive of the legs—to serve as the fulcrum between them and the resistance offered on the oar handle—but not swing out too early from its tucked position.

In a boat, the shoulder-throwing syndrome is generally caused by a misguided notion of how to set the blade in the water. You may actually do fine on the ergometer but may exhibit this early back lift in a scull if you "miss water" at the catch (see "The Catch Drill," on page 80). The critical first portion of connection to the water is lost when the shoulders try to set the catch, rowing the blades forward into the water, rather than letting the wrists and forearms reach upward to set the catch on the recovery cycle.

Stiff arms, with the elbows locked, are generally the culprits. The hands and arms must be relaxed as they approach the catch, in order to release the blades quickly and smoothly to the water. They should remain relaxed even as the blades touch the water, so as not to prevent the legs from feeling the connection to the water. Try to feel the catch in your feet, not in your hands.

Shooting the Tail

The opposite syndrome to throwing the shoulders is when your back doesn't initially engage the work of the stroke at all. The legs push down and the seat, or "tail," shoots back, but the shoulders and the oars haven't moved much at all. You will be stuck sitting in a collapsed, bent-over position at mid-drive. In this case, there is a loose linkage between the legs and the back. Again, your body-angle tuck established at the catch position should be maintained through the first half of the drive. This requires that the back, and the lats specifically, support the leg drive.

This is another common linkage problem found among novices, but it also can manifest itself more subtly in the technique of more advanced scullers. A slight slip in the back-to-leg connection can be a sign of a weak back or of too much load on the oars. A lot of pressure goes onto the back in rowing, and shooting the tail is often the body's attempt to take the pressure off itself.

Breaking the Arms Early

Another common upper-body fault is to start pulling the arms in at the commencement of the drive, before the legs or the back have had a chance to move the oars. This problem can manifest itself in novice and advanced scullers, especially when the water conditions get rough. Because we use our hands and arms much more consciously in our daily lives than we do our legs and feet, they are always trying to take control (particularly when things feel unstable). Part of learning how to scull is re-educating the upper body, teaching it to relax and work in conjunction with the legs.

Using the arms early gives the sense of adding more power to the stroke, but it has two negative consequences. First, it generally denies the legs and back their full impact on the oars. Second, it leaves the finish of the stroke rough.

For novice scullers, early arm break is generally something that gradually disappears as one gets more comfortable in the boat and builds up strength in the arms. Long rows that eventually tire the arms and force them to relax are often instructive. One cause of early arm break may be a weak or injured back. The arms act to shield it from the full strain of the stroke. Building up the back muscles, letting them heal if they are injured, and/or adjusting the posture to a more upright catch position are common solutions to this problem.

The Backswing Stall

The backswing stall, or two-part backswing, is a more subtle repercussion of the early-arm-break syndrome. It usually plagues more advanced scullers who have weaned themselves away from setting the arms in motion early but are still so tense with their arms that they don't effectively hang on the oar handles and therefore can't effectively employ their backswing to help them carry the oars through the middle portion of the drive. Their arms aren't breaking early, but they are tense and restrictive in their connection to the back. Stiff shoulders are often a signal of this problem.

What you see when you look at this type of stroke is a good leg drive, a partial opening of the back to vertical, and then a stop or stall of the back as the arms try to bring in the oars. When the oars are brought in a little with the arms, the back then finishes traveling into the bow. As their legs are driven down, they are substituting a feeling of resistance in the lat muscles for a tightness in the arms and the shoulders. The back, as a result, is underemployed through the second half of the stroke. There is very little backswing to help maintain power.

Once the shoulders start swinging at the conclusion of the leg drive, they should continue moving toward the bow right through to the end of the stroke, without pause or interruption from the arms. Keep in mind that if you can't release adequate tension in the arms, you may be shielding a weak back. You may also be rowing in a shell that is too unstable. Try doing some dryland back-strengthening exercises that develop the back and shoulder muscles (bench rows, bent-over rows, pull-ups, lat pulls, etc.), and focus on some "pick drill" exercises on the water. Also, check the rig to make sure it isn't too heavy.

Throwing the Shoulders (Late Drive)

What happens during mid-drive if a rower has a strong enough back but weak arms? At this same critical junction of the drive, where the arms are scheduled to take over the brunt of the stroke, a weak-armed rower may keep the oars moving with the back, delaying the use of the arms. Naturally, the later the arms are used, the later the back will finish swinging. Excessive backswing not only tends to drive the bow of the boat down into the water, but it also makes things difficult for you around the finish. From such an overextended layback position, it is hard to gracefully come forward for the next stroke without pulling with the feet and subsequently checking the boat.

Overzealous backswingers aren't always endowed with weak arms; they may have just learned to generate power this way. One of the better drills for this syndrome is the feet-out-of-the-footstretchers drill mentioned earlier in this chapter. Rowing with the feet unanchored like this makes a hyperextended layback impossible. Since many rowers are guilty of this technical error, I generally suggest to my scullers that they do their warm-up routines with their feet out of the shoes. If you do suspect weak arms, test yourself with a bench-pull type of exercise. A short-term, specific weight-lifting routine like this will not only strengthen an underdeveloped part of your body but make you more aware of its use in your rowing.

COMMON FLOW PROBLEMS IN THE RECOVERY CYCLE

On the recovery, an off sequencing of the arms, back, and legs can disturb or check the continued motion of the boat through the water. While your early sculling career is generally spent focusing on the mechanics of the drive and how to make it more powerful, the subtle effects of a relaxed, fluid recovery motion can have a profound impact on both the quality of that power and how well it is sustained.

Getting Stuck in the Bow

When you first learn how to row, you are taught various freeze-frame postures to ingrain the basic body mechanics of rowing. Coming out of the bow, for example, you learn that the arms extend first, then the shoulders and back are drawn forward, followed by the lifting of the knees. The arms, back, and legs sequence is indeed

THE LEG-DRIVE DRILL

The leg-drive drill is used to help remedy the premature use of the upper body during the early drive. It is generally used with more advanced scullers who have developed one of the above syndromes, and it requires that the practitioner has already mastered good blade technique around the catch and finish transitions. Even if you're a fairly experienced sculler, it is sometimes a good idea to preface this drill with the catch drill to make sure that you're not late with the blades or sitting at the catch in a badly postured position.

By isolating the stroke to the first half to three-quarters of the leg drive, you can practice keeping the upper-body carriage (including the arms) locked and linked together—offering resistance and feeling the "hang" with the lat muscles, but not opening the back or breaking the arms. At first, the choppy half stroke that is generated will feel odd and clumsy; it is difficult to get the blades out of the water with the arms straight. After you adjust to the initial awkwardness, however, you'll be surprised at how much you can move the boat with just the legs.

The next part of the drill is particularly good if you find you like to break the arms too early. Lengthen the leg drive to nearly full extension and allow the back to swing out slightly to an almost vertical position. This point is where the arms should start pulling, but here the drill ends and the oars are taken out of the water with straight but relaxed arms.

The last part of the drill is tailored to those who like to throw the back late. Start the drill as before, with a good catch connection and send with the legs. Let the back open to vertical, but finish the drive by letting the back and the oars drift gently into the finish position. While the back floats gently into place, let the momentum of the first part of the drive carry the oars into your waist and out away for the next stroke.

important, but it need not be so mechanical once you have learned it well. If you watch Olympic scullers, in fact, you'll generally see very few points in their body motion where they completely stop. The body is always moving, just like on the drive.

Generally speaking, stops or breaks in technique are counter-productive to the forward motion of the boat. Perhaps the most commonly accepted stopping point of the stroke is at the conclusion of the drive, when the body has stopped swinging and the blades have just come out of the water. For most scullers, this is the most natural resting spot in the stroke cycle, and it is initially valuable for beginners to pause here in order to work on balance and basic posture. It is also endemic to team rowing, where such a finish pause makes a group rhythm easier to achieve and sustain.

In advanced single sculling, however, it is important to begin to work on unfreezing this position in the upper body and realizing that even though the seat may briefly stop moving as the legs finish the drive, the hands, arms, and shoulders do not. They are already initiating the first part of the recovery.

Throwing the Hands

Generally, the first awareness you make toward a smooth release of the body out of the bow is the continuous movement of the hands around the waist and out over the knees. Unfortunately, many people interpret the command "fast hands away" to mean an acceleration of the hands into and away from the waist with a sudden halt at the knees. This maneuver, however, still will leave you sitting in the bow. The trick is to get not only the hands around and out of the bow without pause but the body as well.

Instead, the oar handles should be brought around the finish in a relaxed, even manner, traveling away from the body at the same speed they approach it. Rather than thrusting them away from your waist, think of smoothly redirecting their line of travel by circumscribing a small circle. Once the arms are away from the waist, before they even reach the knees, they should pick up the shoulders and bring them out of the bow. This means that the arms aren't fully "locked out" or extended before the shoulders start moving toward the stern. It is a bad idea to ever completely lock the arms at the elbow joint, because you then give up some of the relaxation and resiliency in the arms.

THE HALF-SLIDE PAUSE DRILL

As the name implies, this pause drill focuses on gathering the stroke and balancing the boat at the point in the recovery when the seat has traveled halfway to the front stops. It is particularly helpful for intermediate scullers who need to practice collecting their stroke here, at the half-slide position, rather than right in their lap. Maintaining the body-over position achieved in the body-over pause drill (see chapter 3), gently lift your knees until the oar handles have just swung free of each other and the ends of the grips are nearly butted up against each other.

As you will discover, this drill is the most difficult of all the pause drills, because of the unanchored feeling of your body at half-slide and the precarious balance caused by the folding of your oars in toward the boat. When you attempt the drill and gain some mastery of it, you'll see how easy it is to check the glide of the boat, or to falter with your balance, as you try to move in and out of the half-slide stopping point.

In addition to being a balance drill, this exercise is an excellent way to learn how to get out of the bow and gracefully allow your seat to move into the stern. The half-slide pause and the body-over pause are also somewhat valuable prerequisites in learning how to smoothly transition out of the finish position with the body. If you jerk your hands forward, out over your knees, or pivot at the waist by lunging forward, you'll soon feel how disruptive these movements are to maintaining both balance and run.

Lunging with the Back

The second part of learning how to get smoothly out of the bow concerns the timing of the back and the legs. More specifically, how far over does the back need to be before the legs can start to lift and release? Keep in mind that your primary goal in getting out of the bow is to quickly and smoothly get the weight of the body forward from its stopped position. Again, when many people first learn how to row, especially on high school or college teams, they are taught rigid structural relationships on the recovery with a sense of a stop in between each movement. Hands go away, stop. Body leans over, stop. Legs lift, stop. Catch and drive.

Just as you do not want to throw the hands away from the body and then have them abruptly stop, the back doesn't need to achieve its full body angle before the legs are released. Most people, in fact, don't have the hamstring flexibility to bend forward all the way and keep their legs completely flat. Moreover, holding this position prematurely tenses the lower back and makes it more difficult to stay poised and relaxed with the upper body. Often the legs are released and the body falls or lunges forward to the catch, with little slide control.

Instead, bend forward at the waist and let the legs start lifting as the back gets just past vertical. Let it continue to bend so that it has achieved the amount of body angle you want by the half-slide position of the stroke. Let your back be your guide here. You always want to be sitting in a poised but relaxed posture that allows you to maintain a centered, controlled feeling on the seat. The half-slide pause drill is an excellent one with which to work on combining flow and structure—the flow out of the bow and the setup of the upper-body structure for the upcoming catch.

Falling over the Knees

A last-minute lunge of the back right before the catch sometimes occurs if the upper body isn't poised and ready to change directions at the same moment the seat stops moving. By virtue of having either poor flexibility or inadequate lower-back strength, some scullers don't achieve their full-body angle until they are literally at the catch. Their seat stops moving, but they are still including forward with the back and shoulders, trying to get more reach before the blades touch the water.

Even more so than a pause at the finish, it hurts the boat's glide if the seat comes to a full halt at the front stops and the sculler's body isn't ready. The shell is at the very end of its run, and will register any such disturbance or hesitation with more severe consequences. Lunging not only stops the flow of your own body movements but it throws check against the boat's glide, and buries the stern down in the water.

Strength and flexibility issues aside, the way to work on falling forward is to practice the sculler's half-slide pause drill mentioned earlier in this chapter. Pay particular attention to the latter half of the drill, in terms of both posture and slide control. First, make sure that at the half-slide pause position you have already achieved nearly all of your upper-body angle. Next, as you slide forward to take the catch, force your seat to travel very slowly while you maintain your upper-body position and square up your blades. Keep your focus on the movement of the seat, so that when it stops moving you feel your blades, body, and seat change directions simultaneously, without hesitation.

A FINAL WORD

All scullers exhibit slightly different ways of rowing vis-à-vis their power application, rhythm, use of the upper body, and so on. While there are some basic structural principles to teach and work from, there is also a real danger in trying to pigeonhole your own technique to make it fit an ideal picture of aesthetic perfection. Few scullers row perfectly in the eyes of a coach; the real perfection lies somewhere in between the coach's ideal and the realistic ability of the individual practitioner. This doesn't excuse a quirky rowing style, but it is an allowance that I think every coach and every sculler has to accept. For almost all of the indelicate interpretations of structural style listed in this chapter, a sculler could probably be found who went fast performing one of them. But perhaps they could have gone faster, or at least rowed more injury-free, in the long run.

Former national team sculler, Cecile Ulbrich, out training in her single on the Schuylkill.

CHAPTER 7

RACING

In racing, as in painting, no stroke can be repeated.

—Barbara Green, masters sculler

Even if you aren't naturally competitive, at some point in your sculling career you will probably become curious about racing, if only as a means to test and improve your skills in relation to others. Racing can be an exhilarating experience pushing you to your physical and mental limits, or a harrowing one leaving you ready to chuck it all and never take another stroke again. Reaping the rewards that racing can provide lies in adequate mental and physical preparation and in keeping a balanced view of competition in mind.

To Compete or Not to Compete: The Competitor Within

Most books written about rowing or other sports assume that the reader will eventually want to enter competitions, and that racing represents the natural course of development for any rower. Likewise, within the invisible hierarchy of the sport, the successful competitors are held in the highest esteem and as those whom everyone else should emulate. While I encourage racing and competition as a test of skill and a way to develop, there are certain things to keep in mind.

Most important is the knowledge that the ultimate competition lies within and can't always be accurately measured in relation to others. If you rely on rating yourself based primarily on race results, it can be unhealthy, whether you win or lose. For the perennial losers, the impact is obvious; for the obsessive winners, defeat is sometimes merely suspended. Inevitably, with successful but unbridled competitive fire comes the difficulty of retreat, of gracefully stepping down from the platform and back onto the water to row for rowing's sake. If the focus is always on competition, it can ruin the sheer pleasure of rowing for its own inherent rewards.

Having said all that, let me also say that you shouldn't shy away from competing. Racing can be an excellent way to set short-term goals for yourself, to sharpen your skills, and to push yourself past your self-imposed limits. It is also a way to expose yourself to the sense of camaraderie among other scullers. To shun the competitive side of sculling entirely is to deprive yourself of some very important aspects of the sport.

Are You Ready? Avoiding First-Race Disaster

How do you know if you are ready to start competing? Confidence is a natural prerequisite, and it generally goes hand-in-hand with increasing physical prowess. When you start passing some people out on the river during informal brushes, you may begin to wonder just how fast you can go. However, before you enter the competitive arena, there are a few things you should know, particularly in the area of self-reliance. As a racer, you will have to make sure that your equipment is correctly set and secure, that your training is tailored to the specific event you wish to enter, and that you know all the rules and regulations of the race. It also means knowing a little bit about the competitive field you are going up against and where you fit into it. But don't despair—you're just starting to learn the game. Just be persistent and try to get something of value from every race you enter.

In terms of choosing your race, unless you are indeed a sculling wunderkind, it doesn't make any sense to enter a major regatta until you have tested yourself in several smaller local races, where the going is generally easier. These races are confidence builders, but they are also valuable learning experiences so that when you enter the big one, where you are flying past all your friends and relatives on the shore, you aren't going to embarrass yourself by hitting a bridge. (Actually, there is no guarantee against that, but you can certainly better the odds.)

TYPES OF SCULLING RACES

The small boat races that helped popularize the sport of rowing in the nineteenth century were usually five-mile "stake" races—out and back around a buoy. The famous Thomas Eakins painting *The Biglin Brothers Turning the Stake* shows them at the halfway point in a race, adroitly maneuvering their pair around a small buoy. The value of this type of race was partly for the spectator, who could sit in one cozy location and see both the start and the finish of the race.

The length of the race also emphasized the fact that rowers indeed needed to be well-conditioned athletes. With the demise of the professional scullers and the rise of amateur collegiate and Olympic team boat racing in the twentieth century, shorter point-to-point sprints over 1,000 or 2,000 meters, where boats were separated into individual lanes, eventually became the standard for international competition. For the competitive sculler today, both sprints and endurance racing are available, and each requires its own set of training, racing strategy, and boat skills.

Open-Water and Recreational Racing

One of the most easily accessible venues for shell racing lies in the various recreational regattas held on lakes, bays, and rivers around the country, primarily for wherry and comp class boats. Don't be deceived by the recreational designation. Many of the people who compete in these races are seasoned scullers simply looking to row on a more challenging water surface. In addition to the rougher water conditions, most of the races tend to be long-distance efforts, well exceeding the three-mile mark of a classic river race. In this respect, recreational races are a great way to build endurance, row over a more exotic waterway, and meet other rowing enthusiasts, who generally care just as much about camaraderie as they do about winning.

Perhaps the largest sponsor of recreational races is the **Alden Ocean Shell Association** in Eliot, Maine, makers of the popular Alden Ocean Shell. While many of the Alden-sponsored races are restricted to the Alden-class boats (for instance, the popular **Isles of Shoals Regatta** held every July in Maine), some are open to all comers. The **Ernestine Bayer Memorial Race,** which leads off the Head of the Charles in Cambridge, Massachusetts, every year, includes recreational boats of all makes and classes. Those looking for a more marathon-length test may want to try the annual **Blackburn Challenge,** a twenty-mile circumnavigation of Cape Anne, in Gloucester, Massachusetts.

On the West Coast, open-water rowing is taken even more seriously as an alternative to the traditional sculling done on flat water in narrow boats. Clubs like the **Open Water Rowing Center,** in Sausalito, California, cater to this wilder, more adventurous pursuit. Those looking for the ultimate open-water challenge may want to check out the **Great Catalina to Marina del Rey Rowing and Paddling Derby,** held every October and sponsored by the California Yacht Club. The race is thirty-seven nautical miles and takes some five to seven hours to complete.

Head-Style Racing

Perhaps the best introduction to river racing lies in **head races,** which are generally more informal, staggered-start races over distances of between two and four miles. Scullers and crews are sent off one at a time, every fifteen to thirty seconds, and race against the clock. Since everyone is vying for the best, if not the shortest, course, some maneuvering and passing does take place. This requires strategy and considerable steering ability. The longer distance allows for a modest **stroke rating** of twenty-six to thirty-one strokes per minute (spm), depending on one's fitness and sculling style. In their general character, these races tend to resemble the popular "road races" in which distance runners partake, with some après-race shoulder rubbing, T-shirts, prizes, and libations.

In the United States, head races take place largely in the late summer and fall, providing a racing and social venue for what is still largely considered the off-season for collegiate crews. The largest of its type is the world-famous **Head of the Charles Regatta** held in mid-October in Boston, and styled after the famous Head of the River races in England. Because most head races are not held over straight courses and often travel up twisty rivers, locals and veterans of the race have a distinct advantage over first-timers and out-of-towners. If you can, it is always good to get in a practice row over the course, taking note of important landmarks, buoys, traffic regulations, and the like, which might otherwise surprise you come race day.

Sprint Racing

Sprint racing is what you see during the Olympic rowing events: 2,000 meter side-by-side racing over a six-lane course. Unlike head racing, where you should be focused on your own performance, in sprints part of your awareness has to be on the other boats to ensure your success. In crew, the coxswain serves as the eyes of the boat, letting her team know where the other crews are and deciding when to make a move. In a single, you have to call the shots and devise a prerace plan that you can work during the competition.

In terms of technical skills, unlike head races, where you steer around numerous corners, in sprints you have to hold a straight course with no one in front or behind to guide you. This is generally harder for most people to do, especially given the intensity and speed of the shorter event. You must also learn how to do a racing start and a closing sprint, which will challenge your rowing skills and your cardiovascular fitness. Lastly, the psychology of sprint racing is more intense, because your competition is right beside you. You can't hide on a sprint field. You may find you thrive on this intense competition, and it may bring out the best in your abilities.

TRAINING TO RACE: STRATEGIES AND SKILLS

If you've been training largely on your own, a critical step in becoming more competitive is to join or create a sculling group. Ideally it should be made up of like-minded people who aren't dramatically far off in terms of speed and experience. Training a few times a week in such a group and working at different competitive pieces or set distances is invaluable, especially if these sessions are supervised by a coach. What the group does depends largely on its experience and goals. It may just mean going out for a long tour together to get exercise, build endurance, and enjoy one another's company.

Small groups (ten or less) with a variety of experience levels generally benefit from the longer training that leads to head racing, where everyone can start in a staggered fashion and practice passing one another and getting passed. This is good practice for learning to negotiate the river and your stroke amid the distracting chaos of several other scullers. Generally, the slower scullers will lead off the piece, which will last anywhere from nine to twenty minutes. The theory here is that by starting the slower scullers first, everyone (except the lead sculler!) should have the opportunity to pass another boat.

Strategies and Skills for Head Racing

In head racing it is especially important to keep in mind that you are ultimately racing against the clock and you need to pace yourself based on your *own* physical abilities. It is easy to get excited and caught up in small passing battles with other scullers during the course of the race, but you shouldn't row your race based solely on what other people are doing. If you do, you may lose sight of your own pace and either overextend yourself early on or take things too easy. On the other hand, once you become a seasoned head racer and get placed right in front of someone who you frequently train or race against, you can certainly use them to help push yourself along to your ultimate performance. Starting just ahead of someone slightly faster than you or someone who knows the course better than you do can be a real boon. Even then, however, trying to gauge yourself against another sculler during the course of the race can be dangerous.

The group rowing practices suggested earlier, where you learn how to pass, yield, go around turns and through bridges with other scullers without getting rattled, are perhaps the best training for head racing. Different race situations that require quick thinking and strategy will arise naturally during these sessions. The more you expose yourself to these situations, the more adept and comfortable you will become at handling them.

In a way, learning how to head-race is like learning how to drive a car during a moderately trafficked commuter rush. With some thoughtful maneuvering, you should be able to sail through in reasonable condition in most cases. You'll need to pick up new techniques, such as how to call out to other competitors who either don't see you or won't move, directing them or telling them where you want to go. A cooperative effort—for example, where both scullers work their way under a bridge unscathed—is generally preferable to a clash, which wastes valuable time, damages equipment, and may even cause bodily harm.

Strategies and Skills for Sprint Racing

Again, training with others at least a few times a week is essential to becoming a better racer. To train for sprint racing, which is done side by side in lanes, a smaller, more homogeneous group of no more than four to six is ideal. If you don't have a coach and you row on a busy waterway, be very careful running this type of side-by-side practice with a group. It can be extremely dangerous. Instead of placing everyone side by side, try partnering up and sprinting off in pairs, staggering the starts of each pair. Switch off with different partners, so that everyone gets a chance to race each other.

The first thing you need to know how to do in a sprint race is a **racing start**, a short burst of quick strokes that bring your boat from a dead stop up to racing speed. There are many variations of starts and you should feel free to experiment and develop your own special sequence of strokes, but a general plan is to take five short strokes (e.g., two at half power, two at three-quarters power, and one at full power), followed by ten to fifteen *accelerating* full strokes. By accelerating I mean that the strokes get faster and faster as you near the end of the racing-start sequence, with little regard for the normal rules of slide control. Your ratio of the drive to the recovery off the line will be one to one at best, and during a sprint race it will be closer to one to one than the one to two used in long-distance training and distance racing.

It takes a lot of practice to execute a good racing start, because the body and the blades are moving so quickly. Initially you should practice starts slowly, at less than full pressure, to get used to this quickness. Try the first five strokes at half pressure a few times; then try them with a little more power without losing the flow of the catch and finish transitions. Now add the next ten or fifteen strokes, again beginning by rowing easily at half pressure.

Strive for technical perfection and relaxation in these starts, because a misplaced stroke or **crab** can cost you the race. In regard to smooth body movement, you should master the elements of getting out of the bow (see chapter 6, "Structure and Flow"). *When you think you have these skills mastered, try doing racing starts with your feet out of the shoes.* At first you'll find it unsettling, but once you get the hang of it and put your feet back in the shoes, you should be able to achieve a faster, more fluid start.

The ten or so strokes after your start is known as the **settle.** This is where you want to shift gears and find a pace that you can sustain for the body of the race. To do this, you have to reinstate your slide control and fall into a rhythm and reasonable stroke rating based on your fitness level. If you don't, you'll just end up spinning your wheels, rowing a high rating that doesn't actually have much power to it. Stroke ratings for sprint races can fall anywhere between thirty-three and thirty-six, with racing starts and closing sprints peaking near forty. A **closing sprint** is usually executed during the last ten to twenty strokes of the race, when necessary. If you are out in front of the field, you can hold back your sprint until you truly need it. If you are behind nearing the finish, you may choose to sprint early. You have to gauge your own energy.

Depending on the width of the course, from two to six racers compete at a time in a sprint race, with different heats deciding who will advance to the final race. While some smaller races dispense with preliminary heats, the larger races generally have them, and this multiple-race format factors heavily in the strategy and training for the event. Basically, while you have to row hard enough to qualify for the final, you should try to avoid blowing yourself out in the heats and then having nothing left to give for the final.

Practice multiple interval pieces with other scullers to determine some of your strengths and weaknesses: how well you get off the line, how well you can row through someone or hold off someone trying to row through you, how well you can sprint. The more you can rehearse these scenarios, the better prepared for them you will be. Have a stronger sculler start behind you and learn how to hold him or her back without going over the edge of your fitness and technical ability. Have a slower sculler start ahead of you and work through him or her with the same integrity.

In many ways, even though it lacks the potential contact of the head race, a sprint requires a more intense effort from the sculler. Physiologically, a sprint race requires a much finer negotiation of one's aerobic and anaerobic metabolic processes and, with this, a deeper level of pain. The only solace is that the race is over much sooner, but somehow time becomes rather irrelevant when faced with burning quadriceps. Part of the pain is incurred in the racing start and in the closing sprint, where the stroke rating is taken up. Both require extra bladework skill and are more taxing physiologically, which is the next topic for this chapter.

ROWING PHYSIOLOGY AND ITS USE IN TRAINING

In the 1970s great strides were made in terms of understanding the **physiology of rowing,** the process of transporting and utilizing oxygen through the lungs, the heart, and the muscles. Thor Nilsen, the Italian National Team technical director, and his disciple Kris Korzeniowski, former coach of the U.S., Chinese, Polish, and Dutch national rowing teams, were largely responsible for spreading the word of these discoveries and subsequently applying them to the world of competitive rowing.

Where formerly rowers conceived their workouts in general terms of duration, intensity, and physical benefit, the new physiology brought with it a more precise vocabulary and a focus on the development of the heart muscle as the key means to realizing better performance. Terms like *aerobic* and *anaerobic processes, anaerobic threshold, transportation,* and *utilization* began to issue from the lips of every coach or competitive sculler, and crews were seen stopping suddenly on the river and urgently probing their necks with their fingers.

The Oxygen-Transport System: Lungs, Heart, and Muscle

In rowing physiology, blood is the key: how fast it is being pumped, how much volume is being pumped, how much oxygen it holds, and how well the muscles can use it. Since muscles rely on oxygen to operate, the efficient distribution, or **transportation,** of oxygen-enriched blood via the lungs and the heart is the primary goal here; the secondary goal, of improving how the muscles use it, is known as **utilization.**

As soon as you begin a rowing regimen, your muscles will start to accommodate this new effort you are demanding of them by building additional capillaries and increasing their efficiency. Long-distance rows, where you build muscle endurance, are the best means of encouraging this secondary process. Another benefit of endurance training is that it increases the overall volume of blood in your system, as well as the number of oxygen-carrying red blood cells. In a way, this part of bettering your physiology is a no-brainer; just go out and put in the miles.

As you get in better shape, however, and start pushing yourself harder to see how fast you can go, you'll realize that the limiting factor to sustaining speed seems to lie in getting better "wind." Quite simply, the harder you go, the sooner you run out of breath. This is where it helps to know how to get more oxygen into your cardiovascular system. This process has less to do with your lungs and more to do with your heart and how much blood it can pump out to the muscles. The mechanical workings of the lungs, heart, and muscles are formally called the **oxygen-transport system.**

The lungs take in oxygen and allow it to enter the bloodstream inside of the red blood cells. The heart pumps the blood to the muscles, where it is metabolized, and waste in the form of CO_2 is given back to the red blood cells to bring back to the lungs to expel.

Aerobic Metabolism, Anaerobic Metabolism, and Anaerobic Threshold

This oxygen-distribution system works fairly well during normal operation, or **aerobic metabolism,** which is the process your body uses during long endurance rows. When the work demands are sufficiently increased (i.e., during the start and the finishing sprints of a 2000 meter race), however, the red blood cells become overburdened with waste in the form of **lactic acid.** Lactic acid takes up the space in the blood cells that oxygen normally occupies, and the muscles must now run on a much less efficient process known as **anaerobic ("without oxygen") metabolism.** By preventing enough oxygen from reaching your muscles, lactic acid is responsible for the burning feeling in your quadriceps.

Perhaps the most important discovery of sports physiology and the one that you can take into your training is the discovery of **anaerobic threshold (AT),** the break point at which the oxygen-using system becomes overtaxed. Special interval workouts have been designed that allow the rower to push up to but not beyond this point, after which excessive lactic acid buildup would make **recov-**

ery time excessive. AT workouts have proven to be invaluable in further strengthening the heart and allowing it to pump more blood, and therefore more oxygen, to the muscles. (One AT workout that I've already mentioned is the short pyramid interval, a number of strokes taken very hard, followed by the same number of resting or paddle strokes. The other is a five-minute, submaximum [90 percent] interval, with an equal amount of rest.)

Using Heart-Rate Calculations

Tracking your heart rate can allow you to get a better sense of your own anaerobic threshold. A heart-rate monitor (see chapter 2, "Equipment") can be used to make correlations between the effectiveness and the intensity of the work being performed. A general but less accurate calculation of maximum heart rate (because it doesn't take into consideration individual fitness levels) is to take your age and subtract it from 220; your anaerobic threshold (AT) should operate some 10 beats below this. Thus, if you are fifty years old, your maximum heart rate is approximately $220 - 50 = 170$, and your AT heart rate is $170 - 10 = 160$. A stress test can tell you exactly where your anaerobic threshold should be. Of course, as you get fitter, it will get higher.

Although most experienced rowers can feel when they are about to go over the edge, working with heart-rate measurements can be a useful process to identify baselines.

DEVELOPING A TRAINING PROGRAM FOR RACING

Without getting fanatic about rowing physiology, how can you use it to develop a suitable training program for racing? How many distance workouts and AT workouts should you do, and when? Part of the answer depends on the level of your fitness and how quickly your body can recover from a taxing workout—and part on the type of race you wish to do. Endurance racing and sprint racing each have their own demands, which require different programs of preparation. I suggest entering a number of head races or some of the shorter recreational races before attempting sprint racing, because even though they are considerably longer, head races are generally less demanding and intense.

A General Plan

Whatever your racing goals may be, the general training progression for competition should be based on the following three stages:

1. Develop a mileage base by doing long-distance work.
2. Add medium-length pieces (AT and/or interval work)
3. Add sprint pieces (anaerobic work).

On both a weekly and a seasonal basis, you need to use these three types of workouts in the right proportion with one another, constructing a well-balanced training pyramid. The mileage work serves as the base of the pyramid, providing a strong aerobic foundation for the medium-length AT work and, subsequently, the shorter sprint work.

Training for a Head Race

If you are a newcomer to the sport, without much prior racing experience in distance events, just finishing the twenty- to forty-minute race may be an accomplishment. This means gradually building your stamina up to the race distance and ideally being able to row hard for more than the prescribed race distance. In the early stages of sculling training, the general goal is to accumulate a distance base, from which you can later begin to think about speedwork in an injury-free and technically correct way. Depending on your available time and fitness level, this is also the stage in which to build muscle and endurance through supplemental out-of-the-boat work, discussed below (see "Land Training for Rowing").

Once you can go out at least four to six days a week and cover the course distance, it may be time to start varying your training with the two workouts mentioned in chapter 5: the time-for-distance rowing and the pyramid. Next, when the foundations of your own rowing are secure, supplement this with a long training row with a partner once or twice a week and a group practice twice a week.

Below, I've listed a typical week's training schedule that my scullers follow to train for the fall head racing. It includes three "hard" days of work (Tuesday, Thursday, and Saturday), three "easy" days, and one day off. Again, modify this plan to suit your own needs, adding or subtracting mileage and overall work. Most of the scullers in my group are what I would classify as "upper club level" in ability.

HEAD RACE TRAINING WEEK

Monday

Long, easy row, from 6 to 10 miles, usually done alone or with a paddling partner. Stroke rating held low (20–24 spm); focus on technique and relaxation.

Tuesday

3 × 9 minutes, with 5 minutes rest in between. These 9-minute pieces are done in a small group format and rowed at 70–80 percent effort (AT range). Stroke ratings range from 25 to 30.

Wednesday

Either a repeat of Monday, done with a partner, or a 50-minute time-for-distance row done alone, seeing how much river you can cover in that time period. Stroke rating is modest (22–25 spm), and effort is held to 60–70 percent of maximum. (Nearing the race date, some rowers will add short pyramids onto the end of this workout.)

Thursday

3 × 15 minutes of 20 on, 10 off for the duration of each piece. This is a pyramid-style workout that can be done either alone or with a small group. The 20 strokes "on" are taken at full pressure, to try to push the power and the stroke rating up above race pace (30 spm or better). The 10 off are taken easily, but not sloppily. After each 15-minute piece there is a 5-minute rest.

Friday

Short, easy mileage: 4 to 6 miles on your own.

Saturday

Race day, or race practice. Near maximum effort over the distance to be raced, repeated twice if time and energy allow. For my group this means rowing over the 3-mile Head of the Charles course, preferably racing against people from other clubs. These pickup races are important dress rehearsals for the real thing.

Training for Sprint Racing

To train for 2,000- or 1,000-meter sprints, at least twice a week you will need to incorporate some shorter interval training pieces into your workout program—the kind that bring you up to your anaerobic threshold. These intervals can be two to four minutes in length, with an equal amount of rest in between pieces to allow your body the time it needs to deal with the lactic acid buildup. These should be done at race pace, simulating the physical and mental intensity of a real competition. In terms of length and quantity, begin with what you can handle and still maintain all-out intensity. Remember to try to keep rowing in between these lactate-tolerance pieces instead of stopping cold to rest. It will help your body get rid of the lactic acid more quickly.

These shorter pieces are, of course, painful. I don't think anyone particularly enjoys the way they make you feel. Think of them as necessary innoculations—that will prevent you from getting "sick" on race day.

I have outlined a typical spring or summer training week for my scullers preparing to enter sprint races on the next page. Again, I consider it a modest schedule for competitive club scullers that you should modify to suit your needs.

Time Off, Tapering, and Training Seasons

While discipline and hard work are honorable qualities, you have to be smart in planning how you expend your energies. For most people, every day can't be an all-out effort. Listen to your body and monitor how it reacts to the schedule you lay out for it. If you are constantly exhausted, mentally and/or physically, you can't very well go into a workout or a race with a fresh attack. Many elite athletes take their resting pulse every morning to see if it has returned to its normal range. An elevated pulse means a rest day. Constant fatigue and sore, heavy muscles are the signs of overtraining. A few days before a big race, it is essential to pare down or taper your training to allow yourself an adequate amount of rest.

From day to day, week to week, season to season, you need to balance training and rest and to realize that—despite what the physiologists may say—you are not a machine. Psychologically and physiologically, you need to vary the duration and intensity of your

SPRINT RACE TRAINING WEEK

Monday

Distance row of 4 to 8 miles at 60 percent of maximum effort. Even when you are training to race shorter races, you should try to maintain some mileage.

Tuesday

3 × 9 minutes, with 5 minutes rest in between. Yes, this is the same workout I use in the fall (everyone has their favorite). Remember, it's an AT workout, done at 70–80 percent effort.

Wednesday

3 × 15 minutes of 20 on, 10 off. Same workout as the Thursday fare in the fall, done to get the rating up over short bursts.

Thursday

5 × 5 minutes, with 2 or 3 minutes rest. These are done at 80 percent effort, preferably side by side against an opponent. Ratings range from 26 to 32, depending on fitness. At least some of these are done with a racing start and/or a closing sprint, also to practice these racing skills.

Friday

Practice racing starts. Warm-up row (a few miles), followed by 6–10 1-minute pieces—all done with a racing start. These are short, intense bursts, about 30 strokes long, that allow you to focus on the first part of a race.

Saturday

Race day or 2 × 2,000 meters at 90 percent effort. Find a compatible partner and race side by side, simulating the race distance you'll be doing (it may be more or less than 2,000 meters).

workouts to keep yourself fresh. Some rowers swear by two-week, four-week, or six-week cycles, but the more important point is to create a rowing schedule that allows you to keep coming back for more without burning out. Begin each season with a general plan based on the pyramid model, set a weekly schedule with your coach, and then be prepared to modify it slightly from week to week, adding or subtracting as your fitness dictates.

LAND TRAINING FOR ROWING

During your first season or two in a scull you may not be able to work your muscles as much as you'd like or get your heart rate up to the desired levels. The technical challenges of bladework and balance prevent many enthusiastic novices from driving the stroke rating and power up to race-pace levels. How do you keep in shape or get in better condition while your boat skills are still developing?

Traditionally, competitive rowers have used running, climbing stadiums or stairs, weight lifting, erging, and various circuit calisthenics to further condition their bodies for the sport. In climates where winter forbids rowing, such activities have proven invaluable in not only maintaining and improving cardiovascular fitness but developing specific muscle strength. Another way to look at land training is that it can provide a physical and psychological break from the repetitive grind of rowing. Like any other repetitive sport, rowing overdevelops certain muscles and overlooks others. This can lead to both specific strength and flexibility issues as well as injury. For this reason, your land training should serve to strengthen secondary, or supporting, muscles, such as your abdominal and intercostal muscles (see "Torso Training"), which you don't use in the scull, and should include a daily stretching routine. Books and classes on stretching and/or yoga or Pilates are recommended for this purpose.

Naturally, what you do outside of the boat largely depends on your time and goals. Given only an hour or two a day to exercise, the average sculler would probably be best served to spend that time on the water. As the seasons go by, you will naturally develop the muscles and the endurance you need to effectively move a scull through the water. If you have the extra time, however, or live in a climate that forces you off the water for a few months, you can often bring yourself to a higher level of strength and fitness sooner through the use of these supplemental land exercises. This is particularly true if

TORSO TRAINING

As the legs and the arms get stronger, it is important to keep the muscles in the lower back and front rib cage equally strong. These two areas are otherwise vulnerable to injuries that can put an early end to your rowing career. Take the time to stretch and strengthen the girdle of muscles around the midsection by doing sit-ups, back-ups, side-ups, and torso twists. I suggest the following set of exercises for my own scullers:

1. Sit-ups. Begin on the floor, lying on your back. Bend your knees so your feet are flat on the floor and slowly do 10 to 20 crunches, with your hands resting lightly behind your head or folded across your chest.
2. Side-ups (left). Roll over onto your right side. Set your bottom arm perpendicular to your body to help you maintain balance. Lift your left leg up a foot or so as you bend your torso up toward it simultaneously. Repeat 10 to 15 times.
3. Back-ups. Roll over onto your stomach. Pointing your toes and fingers outward, lift your right hand and left leg up a few inches together and hold for a few seconds. Now do the left hand with the right leg. Repeat 10 to 50 times. (Follow this with 10 push-ups.)
4. Side-ups (right). Roll over onto your left side and do the side-up exercise as before.
5. Torso twists. Roll onto your back again, and get a 10- to 20-pound weight or medicine ball. Hold the weight in both hands equally, extending your arms skyward. Lift your knees up as well. Now lower your hands to one side while you let your knees drop to the opposite direction. You should feel the stretch in your back and stomach. *Do this slowly.* Bring your hands and knees back up to center and then lower them to the opposite side. Repeat 3 to 5 times.

Repeat the entire set of exercises three times.

you have not had other athletic training or are not naturally gifted with strength in certain areas of your body.

PSYCHOLOGY AND MOTIVATION

Before you get too caught up in all the training theory and physiology of rowing, remember that you are not a machine. While it is fun to focus on theory for a while, it can become a little tedious, much like rowing only on an ergometer and tracking the numbers, instead of being out in a shell enjoying the river around you or thinking about the larger picture. Whether you are "in training" or not, you sometimes have to think about what motivates you to row. Is it solely the thrill of competition, the companionship of other rowers, the physical well-being, the enjoyment of being outside on the water? Your intentions are important, especially if you want to train to compete at a high level.

In the middle of anyone's competitive career, as in the middle of every race, there is a break point at which you ask yourself, "What the hell am I doing here?" Training and racing are hard, and therefore your passion has to be as solid as your heart, lungs, and legs. Many top-notch scullers don't fit the physical mold for success: they're too small, not lean enough, technically rough, not

THE INNER GAME: RACING AS PERFORMANCE

In terms of preparing for the intensity of racing, two aspects, the mental and the physical, need to be combined. Mentally, until you actually get out there and start entering regattas, there is no way to adequately describe the added pressure— the prerace jitters, the sleepless night before the race, the false sense of extra power provided by an adrenaline rush. A race is not just another hard "piece," it is a performance. Many people train their bodies hard, but when race day comes, they seem to fall apart in a jumble of tangled nerves. They are so wired that they can't display what they are truly capable of doing.

Naturally, your body has to be trained and ready to show its stuff, but you also have to learn how to identify and deal exceptionally strong. Yet when it comes down to racing, they become transformed and outpull anyone who is put beside them. Technique, size, and lactic acid don't stand in their way; willpower brings them victory.

Some of this may be naturally embedded in a person's character, but some can be developed as part of training by learning to channel thoughts on a specific goal and to mentally prepare for achieving that goal. Another way to look at it is, if all your practices are done with a submaximum mental effort, what do you think the effect will be on race day? The famous sculler Joe Burk trained himself to race all out by figuring out exactly how fast he wanted to go on race day and then allowing himself to train only at that pace. At first, he could do only short pieces with the necessary intensity, but eventually the intervals got longer and longer. His high stroke ratings and early use of the upper body were frowned on by the traditionalists in the sport, particularly by the British, who had to fork over the Diamond Sculls prize that he won in record time in 1938.

I'm not suggesting that everyone train like Joe Burk, but depending on what you want out of rowing, you have to think about developing your mind as much as your body, whether it is toward a competitive goal or one that is more self-measured. The most important reading of the heart can't be taken with a heart-rate monitor.

with some of the demons that may besiege you on your big day. A gradual exposure to racing situations is generally the best method, during practice sessions with another sculler or group of scullers. If you row largely on your own, visualizing other scullers around you and taking strokes with them in your mind is also helpful. On race day, a few hours before your event, try to find a quiet place where you can sit, stand, or lie down and close your eyes to go over a mental plan for the race. It shouldn't be too intricate, but it may include realistic contingencies like reacting to getting passed by another sculler. Some people find it helpful to just relax and focus on breathing deeply and calmly, letting thoughts enter and pass through their minds without paying too much attention to them and maintaining a general sense of focused relaxation.

Checking the rigging—again.

CHAPTER 8

RIGGING

Learn to row the rig, don't rig to row.

—*Calvin Coffey, U.S. National Team oarsman and boatbuilder*

For most rowers the first experience with rigging is a bad one. Some part of the boat's hardware breaks or goes out of whack, rendering the shell unrowable. If it is simply a loose nut on the rigger, fixing it usually isn't a big deal, but if the pitch of one of the oarlocks is off, or the footstretcher loosens up halfway through every row, things can get frustrating. Problems like this are no big deal for an experienced boatman or rigger, but they can send the novice into a state of utter despair.

If you're lucky enough to know a rigger or have a coach who has enough basic rigging and mechanical skills (most of them do by necessity), your immediate worries are over. But at some point in your sculling career, you may not have such a guardian angel at your disposal, so it is wise to try to learn a few things about the workings of your boat. Such knowledge is useful not only in terms of repair and maintenance but for making adjustments to the rig that may make your rowing more comfortable and yield better race performances.

"THE LAW OF DETACHMENT"

The rigging of a boat generally refers to the composition of its hardware: the footstretcher assembly, the seat and tracks, the riggers and oarlocks—all those parts located in the cockpit that are not the hull itself. All of these have been attached to the boat after it was made, and some part of each of these assemblies (feet, seat, and rigger) either moves or can be adjusted. If you keep in mind that anything attached to a boat can also become detached, and that anything adjustable can go out of adjustment, you are already starting to see things from a boatman's perspective. Let's call it the "law of detachment."

Most boats come with a one-year guarantee that generally covers what are called "manufacturer's defects." This loose definition includes only things that break for no apparent reason, not damages incurred when you hit a bridge or a coal barge. Usually, you see this sort of breakage on a boat or a rowing product that is brand-new to the market and largely untested. Therefore, be wary of being the first one to own something "innovative," unless you have the manufacturer's guarantee that you are essentially rowing a prototype that can be returned within a given period of time.

Garden-variety rigging problems and repairs are yours to learn how to handle on your own. Don't despair or get angry. Rigging and fixing your boat can be a fun thing to do, and an activity that in the end gives you more knowledge and confidence in your shell.

CUSTOM RIGGING

Even if you buy a new boat, very few are rigged to your exact specifications. You can give the boat manufacturer some of the important measurements, but in the end you'll probably still have to change a few things anyway. Nevertheless, the better you know what kind of measurements suit you best, the better able you'll be to help them get it within an acceptable range. Some boats don't allow for as much adjustability as others, since many manufacturers figure that most people don't know much about rigging anyway. This becomes a problem if you are built substantially larger or smaller than the person the builder had in mind.

Along these lines, if a boat doesn't come with a lot of adjustability it should be the right size to begin with. Most of the better boat manufacturers offer different hull sizes (lightweight, midweight, and heavyweight), but some sell the "one size fits all" boat. In the latter case, you definitely want to be able to rerig the boat to your liking.

OARLOCK HEIGHT

If you row in a variety of boats, the first difference you may note is that the oar handles tend to finish at different heights somewhere between your waist and chest level. Some may be rigged so low that you can barely get your oars off the water in between strokes and end up hitting your thighs or even the gunwales on the recovery. Others are rigged so high that you have to pull the oar handles up to your chest to keep the blades buried, and they often pop out of the water prematurely.

A boat set with the correct oarlock height measurements should allow you enough clearance to get your blades smoothly off the water at the finish and through the recovery of the stroke, but should also let you pull your oars through the drive at a reasonably low level, no higher than your solar plexus. These parameters assume, of course, that you can handle the boat you're in and keep it well balanced. Many sculling instructors initially begin by giving their students a little more height, and then gradually bring it down as bladework and balancing skills improve.

As with many rigging concerns, height is also somewhat reliant on the style of rowing being espoused. One American sculling style practiced in the 1960s and '70s, for example, called for the lowest possible rig that water conditions and the sculler's skill could afford. The emphasis was on early leg drive, with the upper body held in a tucked position until mid-drive. If you watch some of the European scullers, particularly some of the Germans, you will see a much higher rig and a more upright body position at the catch, which sets the back in motion sooner and relies more on upper-body strength to close off the stroke.

Port and Starboard Allowance

The other height adjustment specific to sculling boats is a slight difference between the port and starboard oarlocks—generally between $\frac{3}{8}$ and $\frac{3}{4}$ of an inch—to allow for some degree of crossover in the middle portion of the drive and the recovery (see chapter 3, "Technique"). Most scullers row left over right, with the starboard oarlock rigged higher, but some European clubs row right over left and have the reverse relationship. Open-water rowers, whose boats are often being pitched around by unruly waves, frequently opt to row with no height difference between the two oarlocks. Consequently, they let their hands cross over, either left over right or right over left, depending on the will of the waves on any given stroke.

Measuring and Adjusting Height

In a single, the height measurement, taken from the bottom of the oarlock to the top of the seat, should run somewhere between 5 and 7 inches (13 to 18 cm). The exact measurement depends on your height sitting in the boat and how much you sink the boat—a function of both your weight and the size of the hull. If you weigh 120 pounds, for example, and you are rowing in a men's midweight hull, the oarlock heights will have to be on the low side. Obviously, you are better off rowing in the appropriate-sized hull, but this isn't always possible. That's where knowing a little about rigging solutions can come in handy.

Height can be measured various ways, depending on the tools you have at your disposal. The low-budget solution is to purchase a four-foot-long level, use it to level off the gunwales, then stick one end of it through the oarlock and suspend the other end across the seat. You may want to lay a second, smaller level across the gunwales to make sure that they stay flat. Now use a tape measure to determine the distance between the bottom edge of the long level and the top of the seat.

When you are doing any measuring, recheck your numbers a few times and make sure that you are placing your tools at the same reference points. In measuring oarlock height, for example, make sure that you lay your level at the same point along the sill of the oarlock each time (it isn't flat; it inclines downward). When you drop the tape measure down to the seat, make sure you rest it against the same place on the seat.

Adjusting Height

To adjust the oarlock height, you should ideally be able to exchange some of the plastic washers that rest below and above your oarlocks and reposition them to raise or lower the oarlock itself. Some boats, however, don't have these washers. Some have height-adjustment holes where the rigger plate attaches to the gunwale; others have a pin that can itself be raised.

Some older boats don't offer any visible way to adjust height. There are two ways to deal with such unadjustable boats. One is to make aluminum plates to seat underneath the oarlock pin, thereby raising it. The other is to loosen the rigger and slide in a plastic shim. To lower height, the shim should be placed in the top portion of the rigger plate; to raise it, the shim should be placed in the lower portion. Such shimming, however, should be done with the understanding that it will also change the tilt of the pin in or away from the boat, known as **outboard pitch** (see "Outboard Pitch," page 117). Therefore, shimming should be employed only as a last-resort method to adjust height, or one in which you are also trying to adjust outboard pitch.

OARLOCK PITCH

The next area of rigging that you may become aware of is pitch, because it can have a rather noticeable effect on the carriage of the blade through the water. When most people talk about pitch, they are referring to the **sternward pitch,** or tilt of the oar toward the stern of the boat (see fig. 1). This small amount (4 to 6 degrees) nevertheless helps the blade hold its shallow but buried course through the water. A shortage of pitch (less than 4 degrees) will cause the blade to dive and subsequently get stuck or "crab" in the water; an excess of pitch (above 7 degrees) will cause the blade to lose its bite, or "wash out."

Sternward pitch is either contained within the oarlock assembly or in the oar itself. In the United States, most oars are made with zero pitch, and therefore any measuring and adjusting is done within the oarlock or to the oarlock pin alone, with the use of a pitch meter. The pitch meter is a simple gauge specific to rowing that can be purchased from a rowing-gear manufacturer. The pitch meter is first zeroed on the gunwale, then held up against the back plate of the oarlock.

Measuring Pitch

Generally this measurement is taken with the oarlock held at mid-drive position, or parallel to the centerline of the boat. Most mod-

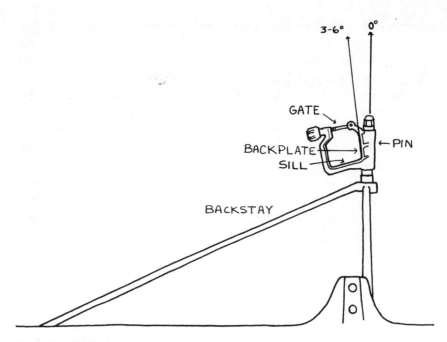

Fig. 1 Oarlock pitch

ern boats allow you to adjust sternward pitch by simply exchanging nicely numbered, cylindrical pitch inserts that fit into the top and bottom of the oarlock, or flat pitch plates that slide into the back face of the oarlock. Again, adjusting older boats is more of an ordeal, involving reseating or shimming the base of the oarlock pin or, in the worst case, actually bending the rigger sill below it to give the pin pitch.

Pitch in Oars

Most American oars don't come with pitch in them, making this an unnecessary concern. Some European oars do contain extra pitch, however, and you need to factor these few extra degrees into your oarlock pitch measurements. If your oars, for example, contain 2 degrees of pitch, you might set your oarlocks to contain 3 degrees of pitch, for a combined total of 5 degrees (see fig. 1 above).

Even if you start with a set of oars containing no pitch, the collars can occasionally shift over time, and the blades can even warp or twist. This will cause the oars to behave strangely in the water, either going too deep or washing out. If you suspect unwanted pitch in your oars, have them remeasured by the manufacturer or try the following test.

Measuring Pitch in Oars

When measuring pitch, you should position the oar horizontally, in a vise or with some large spring clamps. Zero the pitch meter on the flat part of the collar and then butt it vertically against the middle, concave portion of the blade. Even oars purportedly built with no pitch should be checked occasionally to make sure the collars haven't slipped. If you suspect unwanted pitch in one of your oars, you can also measure for absolute pitch (the combined oarlock and oar pitch) by putting your boat in slings, holding the oar firmly against the oarlock, and measuring for this out at the blade. Even though this method theoretically gives you a more exact measure, it is a little tricky to accomplish without two people.

Ultimately, keep in mind that your boat may not sit in the water exactly level to the waterline; the numbers and calculations you make on dry land should be viewed as preliminary measurements. *The real test of rigging is how it feels on the water.*

Outboard Pitch

The other, less frequently discussed type of pitch is called outboard pitch: the tilt of the oarlock pin away from the hull (see fig. 2). Outboard pitch, which generally ranges from 0 to 2 degrees, has a more subtle effect on the carriage of the blade through the water. Some scullers and coaches consider it so negligible that it isn't necessary, and position the pins straight up and down at zero. Others believe that adding a little outboard pitch (1 to 2 degrees) helps keep the blades from diving at the catch (where outboard pitch increases sternward pitch) and hold them more firmly in the water at the finish (where outboard pitch decreases sternward pitch).

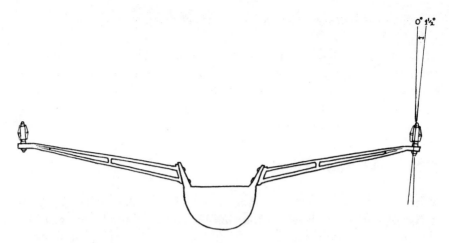

Fig. 2 Outboard pitch

Checking outboard pitch can be done by removing the oarlocks of your boat, leveling the gunwales off, and then holding the pitch meter up against the outer edge of the pin. A quick way to check for outboard pitch without removing the oarlocks is to swing your pitch meter through the positions at the catch, mid-drive, and finish. A boat with no outboard pitch will maintain the same number (5, for example) in all three spots. A boat with 1½ degrees of outboard pitch (the ideal amount, I believe) would give you the numbers 6, 5, 4 (catch, mid-drive, and finish, respectively). A rig with excessive outboard pitch would give you a big spread between the numbers (8, 5, 2, for example).

Again, this effect is so subtle that you might not even notice it until you started playing around with it. What you *will* notice is a boat that has somehow been rigged with negative, or inboard, pitch. If your numbers from catch to finish run from low to high (4, 5, 6, for example), you have a problem. This means that the pins are actually tilting in toward the boat. These numbers will cause the blade to dive at the catch and wash out at the finish. Usually inboard pitch happens only in older boats where someone has added shims between the rigger and the gunwale to boost the oarlock height. Visually, you can almost see inboard tilt of the pins.

Adjusting Outboard Pitch

Many boatbuilders build in the outboard pitch they deem necessary in a single, because it is difficult to adjust without throwing other measurements and rigger fittings out of order. As I mentioned earlier in discussing oarlock height adjustment, the classic (but not the best) way to adjust outboard pitch is to use plastic or metal shims. Slid in between the top of the rigger arm and the gunwale, a shim will incline the entire rigger down and tilt the pin away from the boat. A thin plastic shim, like those used to secure the plastic bag around a loaf of bread, will effect a change of about a degree or so. Unfortunately, it will also lower the oarlock height by about half an inch as well. This adjustment is fine if you needed to lower your oarlock height, but not so good if you had the height all set and just needed to change the outboard pitch.

Some of the fancier boats have adustable rigger sills, where the oarlock pins attach, which allow you to tilt the outboard axis of the pin without affecting height or any other rigging measurement, but this is rare. With some older "fixed" or unadjustable riggers, boatmen would actually bend the rigger sill in a vise or use a homemade "persuader" to do this while the rigger was on the boat, but this practice is not very good for the integrity of the rigger.

FOOTSTRETCHER POSITION

Where do you set your footstretcher? This question has both a short, simple answer and a long, complicated one. I'll try to give you a reasonable compromise. Boats are made with footstretchers that can be slid toward the bow or stern to allow for rowers with different leg lengths. The longer your legs are, the farther away from you, or toward the stern, you'll have to position the footstretchers.

The best way to determine proper positioning of your footstretchers is to check the position of your oars in relation to your waist while sitting at the finish of the stroke. If you have the footstretchers positioned correctly, you should be able to swing the butts of the oar handles free of each other about 5 to 10 inches apart (about a hand's width), depending on how much overlap your oars have. If the footstretcher is too far away, the ends of the oar handles will both be jammed up against your solar plexus, and if the footstretcher is positioned too close, you'll be able to draw the oar handles past your waist without even touching it.

Through the Pin

The second part of footstretcher adjustment is a little more complicated, but it's an important one for those who want to compete and get the most out of their boat. Measuring how far your seat is "through the pin" or "through the work" is done at the catch position, in relation to an imaginary line drawn between the oarlock pins (see fig. 3). In a single, this line should cross over the holes of the seat when it is at the forward position. In the olden days of fixed, short tracks, this measurement could be approximated by simply coming forward to the catch and seeing how close to the front stops the wheels of your seat were. In a well-built boat, you wanted to come as near to the front stops as you could without hitting them.

Nowadays most boats are built with adjustable tracks that allow you to slide them forward or back. Using them to calculate where you are in relation to the work is therefore unreliable. Instead, rolling forward to the catch position, you should be able to get your hips nearly through or even with the imaginary line across the pins. This is known as *zero*. In larger, faster boats, you want to be farther through this line and into the stern, to allow for the added speed of the water rushing by the hull. The idea is that the faster the boat is traveling, the harder it is to get the blade set in the water and working for you.

Given that different scullers have different speeds, how do you tell where you should be in relation to the pin line? What I usually suggest to my beginners is that they start conservatively, with the footstretchers close enough to allow plenty of oar-handle clearance around their waist at the finish. Then, as they get more proficient and comfortable with what they are doing with oar handles, I have them move closer and closer to the work, until they reach a point that provides a good purchase on the water at the catch for the particular kind of pieces they are doing (e.g., fast sprints or head racing). If you are too far through the pin in a single, your blades will feel heavy and sluggish at the catch. With this in mind, you may do your warm-up and endurance training with the stretchers one notch closer to you, and your sprint work one click farther away. Experiment.

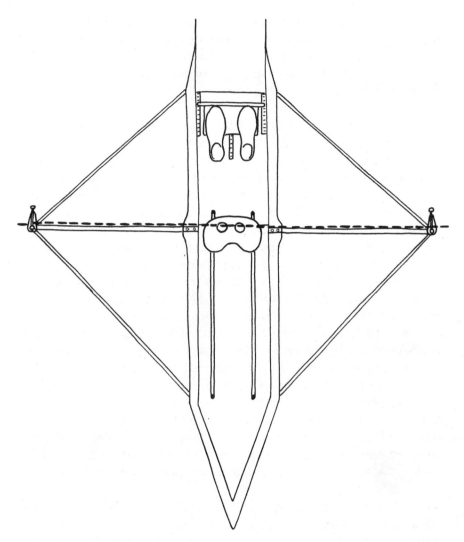

Fig. 3 Through the pin

Heel Height and Footboard Angle

What if you think you've found the best position for your foot-stretchers but you still feel cramped at the catch, unable to get your hips and seat through the pin? You might just have bad hamstring or ankle flexibility. Some rowers do and they have a difficult time getting into a comfortable, relaxed catch position. Stretching may help, of course, but some rigging adjustments can also compensate. In some boats, the height of your heel in relation to your seat and the overall angle of the footstretcher, or footboard, can be adjusted to help you come forward more easily.

The heel height can be calculated by simply resting one end of a short level on the top of the seat and measuring down to the bottom of the heels (see fig. 4). In general, this number should fall between 16 and 18 centimeters (6¼ and 7 inches). If you are taller than average or have particularly long legs, you should rig your boat at the long end of the spectrum; if you are shorter, you should go the other way. In adjustable boats, the shoes or the footboard itself can be lowered. Even in older boats with clogs that aren't adjustable, you can often just drop the heel cup and redrill the screw holes.

Keep in mind that as you drop the heels, you are moving the heels both down and closer to you. This may necessitate a small readjustment of the footstretcher farther away from you.

Another way to allow more comfort at the catch is to flatten the overall footboard angle. Most boats are rigged with the footboard set between 39 and 42 degrees. If you have poor ankle flexibility, you may want to situate them more toward the horizontal. If your boat isn't equipped with this adjustable feature, it may not be worth the trouble. After measuring the footboard with a protractor, you'll have to reposition the board at its two attachment points, the crossbar and the bottom angle plate. Unless you are handy with tools, let a boatman or the boat company help out here.

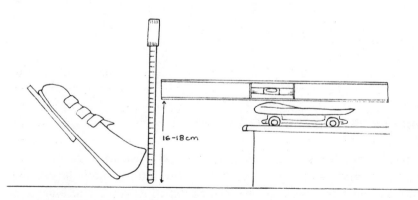

Fig. 4 Heel height and footboard angle

SPREAD, INBOARD, AND OAR LENGTH

Other than the weight of the boat, the overall heaviness or "load" of any given rig is determined by the measurements of oarlock spread, inboard oar length, and overall oar length. In rigging your single, you need to consider these three concerns together to establish a comfortable setup. Again, while there are some general guidelines to follow, you may have to play around a little and experiment to find the ideal settings. These will be based primarily on the way you row, your size and fitness level, and the type of rowing you want to do (racing versus touring).

Measuring and Adjusting Spread

Spread simply refers to the distance between the two oarlock pins. Think of it as the wingspan of your boat. If you run a tape measure from the middle of one pin to the other, you'll get your overall measurement. A good starting point for most scullers is 160 centimeters, or 63 inches. Shorter scullers sometimes favor a shorter spread, and taller rowers a longer one.

When you set the spread for the first time or readjust it, you also should check to make sure that each pin is indeed equidistant from the boat. Most people do this by finding the centerline of the boat and measuring out to the oarlock pin. Thus, if your overall spread is 160 centimeters, the distance of each oarlock from the center of the boat should be half of that, or 80 centimeters.

Measuring and Adjusting Inboard

Inboard is the length of your oar from the end of the handle to the top edge of the button, or collar. The amount of inboard you should have is calculated in tandem with the spread measurement above, so that you end up with a rig that has both the proper amount of load and the correct amount of oar-handle overlap. Generally, overlap should be between 6 and 8 inches. I usually have beginners start with 6 so they have less problem negotiating the crossover and the finish portion of the stroke (see "Crossover" in chapter 3).

When you know how much crossover you want, you can figure out your inboard dimension by simply dividing your spread in half and then adding half of whatever crossover measurement you choose. Thus, if I want to spread my single at 63 inches and have 6 inches of overlap, I divide 63 by 2 and get 31½; then I add half of the desired 6 inches of crossover (6 ÷ 2 = 3). I end up with 31½ + 3 = 34½. This length represents the distance between the end of my oar handle and the top edge of the button. To adjust the button I simply loosen the two screws on either side of the joined plastic ring and slide it into place.

Adjusting Load

Now that I've sketched out the relationship between spread, inboard, and overlap, let's get back to load. Say you've rigged your single with the above measurements but you find they are too heavy, i.e., it takes too much strain to get the oars through the water on the drive. You have three options. If you want to make only a small change, you can just increase your inboard measurement on your oars a little bit. By simply shifting the button a little farther toward the blade, you'll effectively give yourself a longer lever, with which you can move the oars through the water more easily. By "a little" I mean a centimeter or two. Anything more than that will increase the overlap on your oars by an ungainly amount.

If this is still too much load, or you don't like the added crossover caused by merely increasing the inboard, you have another option. Lengthening the spread, done together with a corresponding increase in the inboard dimension, will greatly lighten the load by changing the fulcrum point of the oarlock.

The other effect of doing this, however, is that it causes the oar blade to transcribe a smaller arc through the water. Tightening the spread while shortening the inboard length will have the opposite effect. Some coaches believe that there are optimal arc lengths, or catch and finish angles, that maximize the stroke's efficiency. If you start spreading your rig too far out, you'll have to take a lot of strokes to maintain the same speed as everyone else; if you start tightening up your rig too much, you may start "pinching" the boat at the catch and the finish, where the oars swing in too close to the hull.

Oar Length

A final factor in load is the overall length of your oars. Because of the difficulties I just mentioned above, sometimes a more preferable strategy is to row with a shorter or longer oar to affect load. Especially if you row at a club where the boats are all rigged the same way and can't be changed, you may want to get your own set of adjustable-length oars. They will give you more options when you start playing with rigging.

The standard oar length for macon-style blades is 298 centimeters; for hatchets the length is 290 centimeters. If you are considerably taller or stronger than the average rower, you may want to try a longer oar (300 centimeters for a macon, 292 for a hatchet). If you are on the light side, experiment with a shorter oar (296 centimeters for a macon, 287 for a hatchet). Adjustable oars generally require you to loosen a set screw at the base of the shaft, then slide the handle in or out. When you are doing this, make sure that you adjust your inboard dimension accordingly.

FINAL NOTES FOR RIGGING FANATICS

Most coaches advise beginners to "learn to row the rig" before they start "rigging to row." Until you've put in enough time, rowed many different boats, and established a consistent sense of style, resist the temptation to constantly fiddle with your boat. If you do start messing around with the rigging, keep a log of the changes you make and the effects they have, both in terms of feel and measured speed. That way you can look back and get a better idea of which changes work and which don't. Even the most accomplished sculler can go overboard on rigging and end up going slower.

Putting the boat to rest for the day.

CHAPTER 9

ENDGAME

It's a great art, is rowing.
It's the finest art there is.
It's a symphony of motion.
And when you're rowing well
Why it's nearing perfection—
And when you reach perfection
You're touching the Divine.
It touches the you of you's
Which is your soul.

—George Pocock

If you scull long enough or work with the same group of scullers over an extended period of time, you may find yourself talking less and less about things like technique, training, and rigging and begin to utter some rather strange ideas that fall somewhere in the fields of philosophy, psychology, and religion. Perhaps it's merely an indication of the onset of senility; perhaps it's an effort to express some of the more profound aspects of the sport. On dry land, I get as squeamish and suspicious as most people when others start talking about the spiritual or transcendent aspects of their rowing. Some of this undoubtedly comes from the team oarsmen's unwritten verbal code to communicate as little as possible, preferably through a series of grunts, groans, and minimalist body language. *Don't talk about it, just row.*

There are good rows, however, and there are bad rows. And then there are the rows that can only be described as magical. Everything seems to come together and allow a virtual effortlessness to the motion, one devoid of the usual distracting thoughts about your own physical limitations, complaints about your boat, or worries about how you did against someone else in competition. You are somehow caught up in a wonderful feeling of fluid strokes, smooth boat movement, and connectedness. Call it what you will, these magical moments feel wonderful, and some scullers who aren't ruled by a rigid training agenda might do well to set their sights on reproducing them in their daily rows. Are they just fleeting moments, or can you conjure them on your own?

Competitive or not, most scullers are curious about anything that furthers their performance and their enjoyment of the sport. These goals need not be mutually exclusive. Scullers love to talk about the various details of training and technique but are reluctant to discuss some of the internal motivational aspects that might actually help their rowing if they were articulated. As you go along, and begin to experience the type of magical rows described above, you may want to make them part of your larger rowing goals.

For many people, rowing becomes merely hard work, a silent acceptance of pain and repetitive drudgery all made worthwhile by the promise of victory. Their success in sculling is measured almost solely by how they do against their opponents, not only on race day but on a day-to-day basis against the other members of their club. It's very easy to get caught up in this cycle, because it's so incredibly simple. You row to compete, and you compete to win. Anything less than that is unsatisfactory. The deficiency to this type of mind-set, I believe, is that it caters to dissatisfaction. To get through the rigorous training regime they impose on themselves, these athletes almost have to put on blinders—they have little concern for the fact that they are in a boat on the water, whether the sun is shining or the flowers are blooming. Rowing is merely a vehicle for them to do well in competition.

As I mentioned earlier in this book, competing can be a great way to hone your skills, get in shape, and have some fun at the races. But even if you do become a serious, competitive sculler, you should strive to keep in touch with the roots of your rowing—to reach beyond your dealings with pain, technical excellence, and opponents and toward something a little larger. Silken Laumann, the well-known Canadian single-sculls champion, pehaps said it best:

Rowing is a great teacher. When the medals are old and dusty, my real memories will be of how I found a pureness on a river in a wooden boat, the pureness of a pursuit whose greatest reward is the knowledge that you have tried, and tried with all your might. The strokes down the river teach me. They show me how hard life can be, how long it can take to get what you want, and ironically, how getting what you want is often the least important part of the experience.

I mention all of this because there are so many scullers who want to learn the "tricks" of sculling quickly, either to become fast and win races or simply to avoid the numerous frustrations along the way. The technical information is necessary, to be sure, but in the end technique must be set aside for true grace to be realized. The process of learning and forgetting can't be rushed. When you try to rush it, to hold on to an agenda or goal that you aren't ready for, it takes away from a relaxed presence of mind and simply leads to frustration.

"How long will it take me to learn how to scull?" is the question a beginner always asks. "I'll have you on the water in less than an hour," I assure them. "But it will take years to learn."

FOCUS AND FLOW

Somewhere along the line I began realizing that as my own scullers became better technically, what we started addressing on the water was more and more centered on achieving and sustaining an ephemeral mental-to-physical state of "flow." It all started innocently enough, when I began to notice how some of my more experienced rowers who had achieved technical mastery seemed to fall in and out of this state of grace. Sometimes they would row beautifully, and sometimes, even within the same practice, they would fall back into a rather mechanical or wooden rendering of the same motion. From a technical standpoint their stroke hadn't really changed, but suddenly the scull was not moving along as smoothly or quickly as it had been. Often it looked like they were at odds with the boat, fighting to make it move well. What was happening?

If I really tried, I could put their strokes under a microscope and perhaps identify some trace of an old habit that was rearing its ugly head. The inconsistency seemed to be more of a mental thing— a lack of concentration, of being present with each stroke. But who

Endgame

129

could do that anyway? From my own sculling I knew how difficult, if not impossible, it was to focus on each stroke taken over a sustained period of time. The mental effort is intense, like trying to look straight at the sun.

I also remembered from my days of sweep coaching how I could easily tell if one of my crew members was having an off practice. Their oar would be going in the water at the right time, their body moving with the others, but an elemental spark seemed to be missing from their stroke nevertheless. Usually, if I questioned the individual later, I'd discover that they had an exam coming up, a relationship problem, or some such other external stress. To solve the rowing problem, I found myself trying to help with the personal problem. I did this as a coach, to offer support, but also to try to get their mind back in the boat 100 percent.

The beauty of team rowing is that, at least to some extent, the other members of the crew can psychologically carry the displaced person along for the ride. The rhythm of the rest of the crew tends to override the individual, personal concerns, and take the off-kilter rower back into the group focus to achieve "swing." In a single, however, a lack of focus has a much more profound impact on the movement of the boat. When sweep rowers become scullers, even though they are physically alone, they can often draw from the strength of their past team experience. I knew of rowers who when rowing singles imagine themselves to be still part of a crew, falling into rhythm and drawing energy by conjuring up a mental image of their past team members still around them. What I wondered was, could this sort of mind game be employed to provide a steady, strong focus for the mental demands of sculling?

I began to play with some imagery in my own sculling and pass it along to my scullers. One image was to pretend a large wave was behind the boat. If I kept the right pace, rhythm, and power, I could surf along with less effort, and the challenge lay in staying in the wave and tuning in to the feeling of relaxed flow. Another image was to imagine a rope tied to the bow of the boat and pretend I was being towed along by an invisible powerboat just ahead of me (a wakeless one, of course). Again, the rowing could be quite easy if I kept my strokes perfectly timed, the power even, and the transitions light and quick. What I found with both visualizations was that they provided me with a way to keep focused on my rowing in an indirect, less taxing fashion.

By using an external image like this that synthesized all the elements of my technique, instead of relying solely on my critical, analytic abilities to make constant corrections or adjustments, I found that some of the stiffness disappeared from my strokes. They felt easier, more efficient, and somehow less self-conscious. The mental focus was still present, but the difference between this awareness and one that came solely from trying to make myself row well analytically was indeed profound.

The goal, then, was to get into a more automatic state of mind, where the rowing motion was perceived but not forced or controlled. When I tried these visualizations with some of my better scullers, they initially gave me some strange looks. But when they were able to tap into the imagery, they too felt an immediate difference in the quality of their sculling. "It felt good, but it's confusing," one of them pointed out, "because it's very counterintuitive." In Freudian terms, relinquishing immediate control of the stroke was, in a way, like removing your ego from it. Again, this mental skill isn't all that difficult for a good team rower, who has to blend in with the rest of the boat. But single scullers generally don't think of blending in with anyone or anything. They are often too preoccupied with themselves.

Another sculler, who I was giving a private lesson to, suddenly stopped and said, "It sounds like you're talking about Zen here, Dan." I groaned inwardly, remembering the slew of books in the 1970s that tried to make use of Zen awareness in their subjects, from portraiture to sports—or at least of what Westerners interpreted Zen to be. Zen tennis, Zen skiing, *Zen and the Art of Motorcycle Maintenance*. I instinctively avoided these books, which seemed gimmicky or intellectual in a pretentious way, although I was certainly intrigued by both Zen and Taoism, which strive to do things by "nondoing." The problem as I saw it was semantics. Once you tried to talk about such a concept, it proved elusive.

WATER IS THE ULTIMATE TEACHER

Nearing the completion of this book, I had a wonderful conversation with Shirwin Smith, who runs the Open Water Rowing Center in Sausalito, California. Sherwin had come east to try out some open-water boats made by Chris Maas, and we started talking about the differences between open-water shell construction versus flat-water boatbuilding. After talking for a while about the different attributes of various boats, we naturally drifted into a discussion about some of the differences in rowing technique employed by her open-water rowers—the shorter slide, the higher stroke rating—most of which were dictated by the unique water conditions they faced.

I shared my own rough-water experiences in both sculling and kayaking with her, and admitted that the uneven terrain of the ocean had initially been distressing to someone schooled on smooth water. The "sea change" was just as much a mental one as it was physical—an adjustment of perception as well as an adjustment of technique.

My introduction to open-water rowing was off the shores of Martha's Vineyard, with a friend named Dana Gaines. Dana is part of the small but growing number of open-water rowers on the East Coast, and he has taken his boat through some rough water that many kayakers would prefer to avoid. He once crossed from the Vineyard to Nantucket in a 14-inch-wide Dolphin Rowing Shell, accompanied by my kayaking partner and myself in a double sea kayak. We flipped, accosted by four-foot standing waves, and had to be rescued by a friend in a powerboat. Having lost sight of Dana, we spent the next two hours scouring Nantucket Sound for him. Just as we had given up hope and gone into the Coast Guard station on Nantucket, Dana cruised into the harbor and excused himself for being a little late.

My first row in the ocean was a hard-won revelation. Instead of administering my rigid rowing technique to the water, I had to "listen" and sense what the ocean's surface had to offer, which was different from stroke to stroke. Sometimes my oars would catch the crest of a wave, sometimes a trough, necessitating a change in my handle heights. Or, in beam seas, one oar might catch a crest and the other a trough, pitching the boat slighly over on its side. Initially, I fought with the waves—trying to hold the oars a certain way, to square up at a certain time—to impose my own sense of order upon them. Then I got tired and smartened up. I started listening to the rough water, and let it dictate more of the way my stroke was to be applied.

When I told this story to Shirwin, she nodded, knowingly, and shared her own recent experience of rowing on the flat water of the Charles. It was so effortless, she explained, compared to rough water, that she noticed how easy it was to get lulled into being a little technically complacent. Because the water was so flat and even, her awareness of it was greatly reduced—it almost became like rowing on a rowing machine. "Exactly," I said, pointing out that many river scullers had very little awareness of or regard for the water they were traveling over, in terms of how it influenced the way they should row. Most of them behaved no differently than they would on an ergometer, either looking at their speed meters or keeping very much within their own heads.

What they ultimately needed to develop was this awareness of water and its influence on technique, the very thing that open-water rowers were forced to learn from their first outing. Unlike an erg, you can't just punch or swing at the water as if it were an adversary to be quickly dismissed. Instead, you must consider it in a much more assisting role, as the substance that can help you move forward, by allowing the oars to acts as levers. As long as the oars are in the water on the drive, the boat is moving forward. Enjoy the drive, I explained: go in easily, pull through smoothly, and squeeze off the finish.

In a very simple yet very profound way, the qualities of water influence the nature of technique. The softness of water allows us to enter it at the catch, but when force is applied it becomes quite hard—hard enough to let us lever the boat forward. This is why sometimes, rather than trying to understand things mechanically, it's better to turn one's awareness to the water. It can help break some basic misperceptions and hang-ups. Some of the great swimmers of all time had this "feel for water," a sense of maintaining an even connection to it with their hands. Another kayaking friend expressed it well with this advice: "Think like water."

My own sense is that a sculler's awareness begins in their body and gradually moves outward, through the oars and the boat, and then eventually to the water. You can almost tell what stage of the game someone is at by the way they talk about their rowing. Young rowers are often fascinated by their bodies and how rowing affects them physically. (How was your row? you ask. "Good, but I have a new blister, and my quads ache . . .") Intermediates are often entranced with technique, boats, and rigging, always searching for the magic mix. (How was your row? you ask. "Good, but my rigging isn't quite right, and I think I need a new set of oars . . ."). Still others are obsessed with boat speed. (How was your row? you ask. "Good, but my three-mile time is a little slow . . .")

Older scullers talk about the quality of the water. How was your row? you ask. "The water was beautiful today" is the reply.

GLOSSARY OF COMMON ROWING TERMS

Bow: the front of the boat.

Bow Ball: a protective covering for the bow, usually a rubber ball.

Button: the plastic ring that covers the sleeved midsection of the oar. The button keeps the oar from slipping through the oarlock and butts up against it when in use. The placement of the button also determines the inboard dimension of the oar, and can be adjusted to allow for more or less overlap of the handles.

Catch: the point of the stroke when the oar blades enter the water, marking the end of the recovery and the beginning of the drive.

Check: an interruption in the forward glide of the boat. *Check* can also mean a split or crack in the hull.

Cockpit: the area in a shell that holds the rower and houses the seat, the tracks, and the footstretcher.

Crab: an unpleasant occurrence at the finish of the stroke, when the blade cannot be extracted from the water.

Deck(s): the areas outside the cockpit section of a boat, usually referred to as the bow deck and the stern deck.

Double: a double scull, or two-person sculling boat.

Feather: to turn the blade flat (concave side skyward) between strokes. Feathering is done to lessen the wind and wave resistance against the blade on the recovery.

FISA: the Fédération Internationale des Sociétés d'Aviron, the international governing body of rowing.

Fin: the small piece of metal or plastic attatched to the bottom of the boat to help it track a straight course through the water.

Finish: the part of the stroke where the oar blade is removed from the water, marking the end of the drive and the beginning of the recovery.

Footboard: a strong thin plate or piece of plywood to which the sculler's shoes are atttached. Part of the footstretcher assembly.

Gate: the small bar that closes over the top of the oarlock to prevent the oar from coming out.

Gunwale: the strips of wood or synthetic material that run along the side of the cockpit and prevent waves from entering it.

Keel: the long structural piece that runs along the bottom of a wooden hull, lending a boat longitudinal strength.

Knee: a structural piece of a boat that helps support a traditional rigger assembly. The knees usually also connect the keel, the gunwales, and other structural pieces of a boat.

Layback: the backward lean of the sculler's body at the finish.

Loom: the part of the oar between the blade and the handle.

NAAO: the National Association of Amateur Oarsmen, the governing body of amateur rowing in the United States.

Port: the left side of the boat. Sitting in a scull, this is actually your right because you are sitting backward.

Puddle: a term used to describe the swirl of water left by each stroke.

Quadrascull: a four-person sculling boat, also known as a quad.

Rating: stroke rating, the number of strokes taken per minute.

Recovery: the portion of the stroke when the blades are held out of the water while the sculler readies himself for the next stroke.

Release: another term for the finish of the stroke.

Rhythm: the cadence achieved in a stroke depending on the proportion of time spent on the recovery versus that spent on the drive.

Rib: the structural part of a wooden boat's frame that runs laterally along the inside of the hull.

Rig: the type of rigging arrangement, or dimensions, employed by a rower or a crew.

Rudder: a steering device used in sweep rowing or in larger sculling boats, such as quadrasculls.

Run: the amount of glide achieved by the boat between strokes.

Sculls: generally the term used to refer to sculling oars. *Scull* also refers to a sculling boat.

Single: a single-person sculling boat.

Slide: the seat and track assembly of a boat, which slides back and forth between strokes.

Spacing: the distance between successive sets of puddles.

Starboard: the right side of the boat. Your left, actually, when you are facing backward and rowing.

Stretcher: the footstretcher assembly in a boat, including the clogs or shoes and the means by which they are affixed to the boat.

Stringers: the main horizontal members of a wooden boat's frame, which run along the upper edge of the hull.

Stroke: the general term used to designate a single cycle of the oar. In team boats, *stroke* also refers to the lead rower, whom everyone else follows.

Sweep Rowing: the type of rowing done in pairs, fours, and eights, where each oarsman holds a single twelve-and-a-half-foot-long oar, or sweep.

Swing: the backswing toward the bow during the drive portion of the stroke. In team boats, *swing* also refers to the synchronicity of this movement among the crew.

Washing Out: the premature, unwanted emergence of the oar blade from the water during the drive.

INDEX

Index